Understanding Taoism

*A Beginner's Guide to Discovering Harmony,
Balance, and Inner Peace in the Taoist Faith*

DAVID M. EATON

Contents

CHAPTER 1

Introduction to Taoism

When we think of world religions, we tend to automatically jump to the well-known options, such as Christianity, Judaism, Islam, and Buddhism. But of course, there are more faiths found worldwide, and they are all as valid and as interesting as one another.

In this book, we're going to explore an ancient Chinese faith that may not be one that automatically comes to mind when you think of world religions, but it is a religion with many followers around the world. With mystical roots, we're talking about Taoism.

Taoism, also known as Daoism, is a philosophical and spiritual tradition that originated in ancient China. At its core is the concept of "Tao" (or Dao), which translates to "the way" or "the path." Taoism provides a framework for understanding the fundamental principles that govern the universe and guides followers on how to live in harmony with these principles.

Taoism traces its roots back to ancient China during the Axial Age, around the 6th century BCE. This was a period marked by profound intellectual and spiritual developments, giving rise to various philosophical and religious traditions.

The legendary figure associated with the founding of Taoism is Laozi, often considered the author of the seminal text, the "Tao Te Ching" (Dao De Jing). This sacred book is a collection of 81 short chapters containing poetic and philosophical insights into the nature of the Tao and guidance on living a balanced and virtuous life.

Taoism emphasizes living in harmony with nature and the Tao, embracing simplicity and spontaneity. It challenges conventional notions of morality, emphasizing the relativity of values and the importance of intuitive understanding over rigid rules.

However, Taoism is not just a theoretical philosophy; it offers practical guidance on how followers can cultivate a balanced and fulfilling life. Common practices include meditation, breath control, and other techniques aimed at attuning to the rhythms of the Tao.

Influence on Chinese Culture and Beyond

All major religions leave their mark on society, and Taoism is no different. In fact, Taoism has deeply influenced Chinese culture, leaving its mark on art, literature, medicine, and various aspects of daily life. Even traditional Chinese medicine, with its emphasis on balance and harmony, draws inspiration from Taoist principles.

Over time, Taoism has developed into a multifaceted religious tradition with rituals, ceremonies, and temples. Religious Taoism encompasses a variety of sects and practices aimed at spiritual development, longevity, and the cultivation of inner energy.

In the modern era, Taoism has gained global recognition and has influenced thinkers, artists, and other individuals seeking a holistic approach to life. However, the principles of balance, simplicity, and living in harmony with nature resonate beyond Chinese borders. Taoism represents a philosophical and spiritual tradition that has endured for centuries, offering timeless insights into the nature of existence and the art of living a balanced and meaningful life. Its influence extends far beyond its place of origin, shaping cultural and spiritual landscapes on a global scale.

Historical Context and Key Figures

To continue our introduction to Taoism, let's take a look at some of the key turning points and figures throughout history, starting with the Axial Age:

- **Axial Age (6th Century BCE):** Taoism emerged during a pivotal period known as the Axial Age, around the 6th century BCE. This era witnessed a profound intellectual and spiritual awakening, giving rise to various philosophical and religious movements across different civilizations.

- **Ancient China:** The historical and cultural backdrop of ancient China provided fertile ground for the development of Taoism. The political fragmentation, social upheavals, and philosophical inquiries of the time, contributed to the formation of diverse schools of thought.

- **Confucianism and Daoism:** Taoism developed alongside Confucianism, another influential philosophical tradition in ancient China. While Confucianism focused on social order, morality, and ethical conduct, Taoism explored the mystical and metaphysical aspects of existence, emphasizing the harmony with the natural order.

Key Figures:

Laozi (Lao Tzu)

Laozi is the legendary figure associated with the foundational Taoist text, the "Tao Te Ching." This seminal text serves as the primary source of Taoist wisdom, offering insights into the nature of the Tao and guiding principles for harmonious living.

The historical existence of Laozi remains uncertain, and he is often regarded as a symbolic figure representing the wisdom of Taoism.

Zhuangzi (Chuang Tzu)

Zhuangzi, another key figure in Taoism, contributed significantly to the development of Taoist thought. His work, also titled "Zhuangzi," is a compilation of philosophical dialogues and anecdotes that expand on the principles introduced in the Tao Te Ching.

Zhuangzi's writings explore themes such as relativity, the illusory nature of distinctions, and the concept of "Ziran" (spontaneity or naturalness). His philosophical contributions added depth to Taoist metaphysics and influenced subsequent generations of Taoist thinkers.

Zhang Daoling:

Zhang Daoling is considered a historical figure associated with the development of religious Taoism. During the Han Dynasty (2nd century CE), Zhang Daoling is said to have founded the Way of the Celestial Masters (Tianshi Dao), a religious movement emphasizing ritual practices and the pursuit of immortality.

Zhang Daoling's tradition organized Daoist priests into three hierarchical levels known as the Three Caverns. The movement contributed to the compilation of the Daoist Canon, a collection of sacred texts that form the basis of religious Taoist practices.

The Key Concepts in Taoist Philosophy

Let's briefly look at the key concepts that form the Taoist faith.

Tao (Dao)

Tao is the central and ineffable concept in Taoist philosophy, representing the ultimate principle or source of everything in the universe. It is formless, transcendent, and beyond human comprehension, often described as the unifying force that gives rise to both creation and transformation.

Yin and Yang

Taoism introduces the concept of Yin and Yang, symbolizing the dual nature of reality. Yin represents qualities like receptivity, passivity, and darkness, while Yang embodies activity, assertiveness, and light.

The interplay between these forces reflects the dynamic balance inherent in the cosmos.

Wu Wei (Non-action)

Wu Wei emphasizes living in accordance with the natural flow of the Tao, advocating for spontaneity and uncontrived action. It does not imply complete inactivity but rather encourages actions that arise naturally and effortlessly, in harmony with the Tao.

Ziran (Naturalness)

Ziran embodies the idea of acting in accordance with one's true nature and the natural order of things. It encourages us to embrace simplicity and authenticity, free from artificial constraints.

Relativity of Values

Taoist philosophy challenges conventional notions of good and bad, emphasizing the relativity of values. Actions that are in harmony with the Tao are considered virtuous, while those that disrupt the natural order are deemed unvirtuous.

Nature-Centric View

Taoism advocates living in harmony with the natural world, observing the patterns of nature to understand the Tao. The philosophy promotes a simple and uncluttered lifestyle, appreciating the beauty of the natural order.

Humility and Flexibility

Taoist philosophy encourages humility in the face of the vastness and mystery of the Tao. It emphasizes adaptability and the ability to flow with the changes of life, mirroring the flexible nature of water.

Taoist practices often include meditation and contemplation to explore the depths of consciousness and connect with the Tao. Additionally, some Taoist traditions focus on inner alchemy, seeking to transform and refine the inner energies of the body and mind.

Taoism's Modern and Global Relevance

Taoism's wisdom has transcended cultural boundaries, impacting Western philosophy, psychology, and alternative medicine. Its emphasis on balance, simplicity, and the interconnectedness of all things resonates with individuals seeking a holistic approach to life.

The emphasis on harmony with nature has contributed to contemporary discussions on environmental ethics. Additionally, the principles of Taoism inspire eco-friendly practices and a greater awareness of humanity's connection to the natural world.

Now you know the basics, let's continue our journey into the fascinating world of Taoism.

CHAPTER 2

The Tao – The Way of Nature

B y now, you'll know that the term "Tao" or "Dao" (道) can be translated as "the way" or "the path," and it represents a fundamental concept that encompasses the underlying principle of the universe.

At its core, Tao embodies the idea of harmony and balance, serving as the cosmic order that governs all existence. The concept is deeply rooted in Daoist texts, most notably the "Tao Te Ching," attributed to Laozi, and the "Chuang Tzu," attributed to Zhuangzi. These philosophical works provide insights into understanding the nature of Tao and its application to various aspects of life.

Nature of Tao

Tao is often described as unnameable and formless, transcending human comprehension. It is the source of everything, existing before distinctions between opposites like good and bad, existence and non-existence.

Of course, Taoism also incorporates the Yin-Yang philosophy, where opposing forces are interconnected and complementary. This duality is not about conflict but about the interdependence and balance of these forces.

We then have Wu Wei, which is the principle of non-action or effortless action. It suggests that we should align with the natural flow of the Tao, allowing things to unfold spontaneously rather than forcing them. This can also be done by living in accordance with one's nature or Ziran, embracing spontaneity and simplicity. By letting go of excessive desires and unnecessary complexities, one can align themselves with the Tao.

Water as a Symbol

The analogy of water is often used to explain Tao. Water, despite its soft and yielding nature, has the power to shape landscapes and overcome obstacles. Similarly, we are encouraged to be adaptable and flexible in our approach to life.

As part of Taoism, followers are expected to incorporate a few other aspects. Let's take a brief look at them now...

- **Unity of all things:** Taoism emphasizes the interconnectedness of all things. It encourages us to recognize the unity underlying the diversity in the world, fostering a sense of compassion and empathy.

- **Personal transformation and self-cultivation:** The concept of Tao involves personal transformation and self-cultivation. Followers strive to cultivate virtues such as humility, compassion, and simplicity, aligning their lives with the natural order.

- **Spiritual dimension and transcendence:** Taoism also delves into the spiritual dimension, suggesting that we can attain a state of transcendence by aligning with the Tao. This involves letting go of ego and realizing our interconnectedness with the greater whole.

Exploring the concept of Tao provides wisdom that extends beyond philosophical musings to practical guidance for leading a harmonious and balanced life. It invites us to contemplate the nature of existence, embrace simplicity, and harmonize with the ebb and flow of the cosmic order.

Understanding the Natural Order and Flow

A deep understanding of the natural order is a concept deeply rooted in various philosophical and spiritual traditions. Whether explored through Eastern philosophies like Taoism or Western perspectives such as Stoicism, the idea revolves around recognizing and aligning ourselves with the inherent rhythm and balance of the universe.

At the heart of the natural order is the recognition of interconnectedness. Everything in the universe is intricately linked, forming a web of relationships. This interconnectedness emphasizes that actions in one aspect of life can reverberate throughout the whole.

Of course, nature operates in cycles and rhythms, from the changing seasons to the rising and setting of the sun. Understanding these natural patterns allows us to appreciate the transient nature of circumstances, realizing that challenges, like seasons, are temporary.

In Taoism, the concept of Tao embodies the natural order. Living in harmony with the Tao involves recognizing the spontaneous flow of life and aligning actions with this cosmic rhythm. The idea is to navigate life effortlessly, much like a leaf floating down a stream.

Adapting to this mindset can be challenging at first, but it certainly has several benefits:

- **Decision-making:** Understanding the natural flow aids decision-making. By observing the ebb and flow of life, we can make choices that align with the current circumstances, leading to more harmonious outcomes.

- **Mindfulness and presence:** Cultivating mindfulness and being present in the moment are crucial aspects of grasping the natural flow. This involves paying attention to the present without excessive attachment to the past or anxiety about the future.

- **Acceptance of change:** The natural order includes a constant flux of change. Embracing this reality allows individuals to release resistance to change and view it as a natural part of life's unfolding journey.

- **Learning from challenges:** Challenges are seen as opportunities for growth within the context of the natural order. They provide lessons and contribute to the continuous evolution of individuals.

- **Balance in lifestyle:** Living in harmony with the natural flow involves finding a balance in various aspects of life, including work, relationships, and personal well-being. Striking this balance contributes to overall life satisfaction.

Tao as the Source of Harmony and Balance

Tao is considered the underlying and unifying principle of the universe. Understanding Tao as the source of harmony and balance provides profound insights into the nature of existence, guiding us on a path toward a more harmonious and balanced life.

To achieve harmony and balance, there are a few other aspects to consider:

- **Microcosm and macrocosm:** Taoism states that a person is a microcosm of the larger cosmic order. By cultivating inner harmony and balance, we contribute to the overall balance of the cosmos. Personal cultivation, in this sense, has cosmic implications.

- **Non-Dualistic thinking:** Taoism challenges conventional, dualistic thinking. Instead of seeing opposites as conflicting forces, it encourages embracing paradox and recognizing the interdependence of seemingly contradictory elements.

- **Transcendence and unity:** Taoist practitioners seek to transcend the limitations of the ego and experience unity with the Tao. This spiritual dimension involves realizing that the source of harmony and balance is not only a cosmic principle but also an immanent force within each person.

CHAPTER 3

Yin and Yang – The Dual Nature of Existence

The concept of Yin and Yang is a fundamental idea in Chinese philosophy and cosmology, representing the dualistic nature of existence. This ancient concept has its roots in Taoism, and it has had a profound influence on Chinese thought, medicine, martial arts, and various other aspects of Chinese culture.

The term "Yin and Yang" is derived from the Chinese characters for "dark" (Yin) and "light" (Yang). It is often depicted as a circle divided into two halves, with a smaller circle of the opposite color in each section, symbolizing the dynamic interplay between contrasting forces. The black-and-white swirling symbol is not just a representation of opposites but also signifies the interconnectedness and interdependence of these opposites.

The core idea behind Yin and Yang is the recognition that seemingly opposite or contrasting forces are, in fact, complementary and interconnected. The concept emphasizes the duality inherent in all aspects of existence and suggests that balance and harmony arise from the interaction of these dualities.

The interplay between Yin and Yang is dynamic, with each force containing the seed of the other, symbolizing the constant flow and change in the universe.

Characteristics of Yin and Yang:

1. **Yin:**

- Represents the passive, receptive, and feminine qualities.

- Associated with darkness, cold, stillness, intuition, and the moon.

- Yin is often linked to qualities like introspection, nurturing, and rest.

2. **Yang:**

- Signifies the active, assertive, and masculine qualities.

- Associated with brightness, heat, movement, logic, and the sun.

- Yang is often linked to qualities like ambition, creativity, and outward expression.

Yin and Yang are not fixed entities but rather exist in a state of constant flux and transformation. One cannot exist without the other, and their balance is crucial for harmony and well-being. The concept is not about achieving a static equilibrium but understanding the cyclical nature of change and embracing it. This cyclical nature is often illustrated in the changing seasons, the rise and fall of day and night, and the cyclical patterns of life and death.

The concept of Yin and Yang has practical applications in traditional Chinese medicine, where it is used to understand the balance of vital energy (Qi) in the body. Imbalances between Yin and Yang are believed to lead to illness, and treatments often aim to restore harmony by rebalancing these forces. Additionally, the philosophy of Yin and Yang is integrated into various aspects of Chinese culture, from martial arts to feng shui, influencing a holistic understanding of life.

Understanding Interdependence and Balance

Within Taoism, the interdependence and balance of opposing forces are fundamental principles that guide both thought and action.

The Tao and Interdependence:

1. **The Tao as the Ultimate Reality:**

- The Tao is considered the ultimate reality, an ineffable and unnamable force that transcends human understanding. It is the source and the essence of everything that exists.

- Within the Tao, the concept of Wu Wei, often translated as "non-action" or "effortless action," suggests aligning oneself with the natural flow of the Tao, allowing things to unfold organically.

2. **Yin-Yang Dynamic:**

- The interdependence and balance in Taoism are often represented by the Yin-Yang symbol, reflecting the harmony of opposites. Yin and Yang are not static, but rather dynamic, constantly transforming into each other.

- The Tao Te Ching teaches that embracing both Yin and Yang allows one to understand the whole picture, fostering a more profound sense of harmony and balance.

Balance and Harmony:

1. **Balance of Opposing Forces:**

- Taoism teaches that life is a constant interplay between opposites such as light and dark, good and bad, active and passive. These dualities are not seen as conflicts but as necessary complements to one another.

- The goal is not to eliminate one side in favor of the other but to recognize the interdependence and interconnection between them.

2. **Nature as a Model:**

- Nature serves as a primary model for understanding balance in Taoism. Observing the natural world, Taoists recognize the effortless harmony that exists in the cycles of seasons, the rhythm of day and night, and the interconnectedness of all living things.

- By aligning oneself with nature, individuals can learn to live in harmony with the Tao, allowing life to unfold without unnecessary resistance.

3. **Water as a Symbol:**

- Taoist philosophy often uses water as a metaphor for understanding the principle of interdependence and balance. Water is fluid, adaptable, and, despite its soft nature, has the power to shape and erode landscapes.

- Like water, individuals are encouraged to be flexible and adaptable, understanding that real strength lies in yielding and embracing change.

Personal Transformation:

1. **Wu Wei in Action:**

- Practicing Wu Wei involves acting in accordance with the natural flow of the Tao. It does not imply inaction but rather aligning one's actions with the inherent rhythm of life.

- By practicing Wu Wei, individuals cultivate a sense of spontaneity and learn to respond to situations without imposing unnecessary force.

2. **Simplicity and Detachment:**

- Taoism encourages a simple and uncluttered lifestyle. Detachment from material possessions and ego-driven desires is seen as a way to achieve inner balance and peace.

- The emphasis on simplicity aligns with the idea that excess and overexertion disrupt the natural balance.

Cultivating Virtue and Compassion:

- Taoism places importance on cultivating virtues such as compassion, humility, and kindness. By embracing these virtues, we contribute positively to the interconnected web of existence, fostering harmony in both personal and social spheres.

Ultimately, understanding interdependence and balance in Taoism involves recognizing the dynamic interplay of opposites, aligning oneself with the natural flow of the Tao, and cultivating a sense of balance and harmony in all aspects of life. This philosophy provides a timeless guide for navigating the complexities of existence with grace and wisdom.

Applications in Daily Life and Philosophy

Taoism, as a philosophical and spiritual tradition, offers profound insights that can be applied to various aspects of daily life. Let's explore how Taoist philosophy manifests in practical applications in daily life:

- **Wu Wei (non-action) and effortless action:** In daily tasks and decision-making, we can practice Wu Wei by being attentive to the present moment, making decisions without overthinking, and allowing events to unfold naturally. It involves doing things with a sense of ease and without forcing outcomes.

- **Simplicity and detachment:** Simplifying life involves decluttering both physical and mental spaces. This could mean minimizing material possessions, simplifying daily routines, and letting go of unnecessary worries. By embracing simplicity, we can reduce stress and focus on what truly matters.

- **Nature as a teacher:** Spending time in nature, observing its cycles, and appreciating its beauty can help us connect with the natural rhythm of life. This connection fosters a sense of awe, gratitude, and a deeper understanding of the interconnectedness of all things.

- **Yin and Yang balancing:** Recognizing the presence of opposites in various aspects of life, such as work and rest, activity and stillness, helps us make a conscious effort to maintain balance. For example, balancing periods of intense work with moments of relaxation contributes to overall well-being.

- **Compassion and Virtue:** Practicing compassion in daily interactions, being humble in success, and showing kindness to others align with Taoist values. Cultivating virtues contributes not only to personal well-being but also to the harmony of the larger social and community context.

- **Embracing change:** Embracing change involves adapting to new circumstances without excessive attachment to the status quo. Instead of resisting change, we can learn to flow with the ever-changing nature of life, fostering resilience and a more positive outlook.

- **Mindfulness and presence:** Mindfulness practices, such as meditation or mindful breathing, help us stay present and attentive. Being fully engaged in the present moment enhances awareness, reduces stress, and promotes a sense of inner peace.

- **Humility and constraint:** Cultivating humility involves acknowledging limitations, being open to learning, and avoiding the need to dominate or control situations. By letting go of the urge to force outcomes, we can navigate challenges with greater ease.

To sum up, the practical applications of Taoist philosophy in daily life involve adopting a mindset of simplicity, embracing the natural order, cultivating virtues, and living in harmony with the dynamic interplay of opposites.

CHAPTER 4

The Tao Te Ching – Core Text of Taoism

The Tao Te Ching, often translated as the "Classic of the Way and Virtue" or simply the "Tao Te Ching," is the foundational text of Taoism and, as we know by this point, is a compilation of 81 short chapters that offer profound insights into the nature of existence, human behavior, and the concept of the Tao.

The authorship of the Tao Te Ching is traditionally attributed to Laozi, though historical details about his life are scarce, and his existence has been debated. The historical context in which the text emerged is one of social and political turmoil in ancient China, with many states vying for power and stability. The Tao Te Ching is often seen as a response to the political and moral challenges of the time.

The text addresses various themes, including humility, simplicity, compassion, and the interconnectedness of all things. It provides guidance on effective leadership, the nature of power, and the importance of balance. It encourages Taoist followers to live in harmony with the Tao, promoting a way of life that fosters inner peace and social equilibrium.

Over time, the Tao Te Ching has transcended its cultural and historical origins, finding resonance across different traditions and disciplines. Its verses have been interpreted and adapted by scholars, philosophers, and spiritual seekers worldwide. As a result, its influence extends beyond Taoism, impacting fields such as philosophy, psychology, and leadership studies.

Additionally, due to its complex and poetic language, the Tao Te Ching has been translated into numerous languages, each interpretation bringing its unique perspective. Notable translations include those by scholars like D.C. Lau, Arthur Waley, and Stephen Mitchell. Different interpretations highlight the richness and ambiguity of the original text.

These days, the teachings of the Tao Te Ching continue to be relevant in the modern world. Its emphasis on balance, humility, and adaptability resonates with people seeking meaning and purpose in a rapidly changing and often tumultuous world. The principles of the Tao Te Ching offer timeless insights into the art of living a fulfilling and meaningful life.

Further Analysis of Key Teachings and Principles

The Tao Te Ching's key tenets have been influential not only in the development of Taoism but also in shaping broader philosophical, ethical, and spiritual perspectives. Here's an analysis of some key teachings and principles found in the text:

- **The Tao (The Way):** The concept of the Tao is fundamental to the entire text. The Tao is described as the ultimate principle that encompasses and unifies everything in the universe. We know that it is formless, transcendent, and beyond human comprehension. The Tao is both the source and the destination, and the central idea is to align life with the natural flow of the Tao. This alignment is not about imposing will but rather about attuning ourselves to the inherent harmony of the cosmos.

- **Wu Wei (non-action or effortless action):** Wu Wei is a key principle emphasizing the idea of non-action or effortless action. It encourages us to act spontaneously and in harmony with the natural course of events. It does not advocate for complete inactivity but rather suggests that a person should act without unnecessary effort or resistance, allowing events to unfold naturally. Wu Wei embodies the notion of going with the flow and avoiding unnecessary struggle.

- **Balance and harmony:** The Tao Te Ching stresses the importance of balance in all aspects of life. This balance is not just external but extends to the inner harmony within an individual. The text encourages us to embrace the dualities of existence and find a middle path between extremes. The idea is to avoid excesses and cultivate a state of equilibrium, recognizing that extremes can lead to imbalance and disharmony.

- **Simplicity and humility:** Simplicity is celebrated in the Tao Te Ching. It advises against unnecessary complexity and emphasizes the value of a simple and humble life. Humility, in this context, is about acknowledging our limitations and recognizing the interconnectedness of all things. Through simplicity and humility, we can avoid unnecessary desires and ego-driven pursuits, finding contentment in the present moment.

- **Teaching through paradox:** The Tao Te Ching often employs paradoxical language to convey its teachings. This technique challenges conventional thinking and encourages readers to transcend dualistic perspectives. The use of paradoxes serves to highlight the limitations of language and conceptual understanding, pushing us to contemplate deeper meanings and insights.

- **Leadership and power:** The text provides guidance on effective leadership, advocating for a leadership style that is humble, compassionate, and in harmony with the Tao. True leadership, according to the Tao Te Ching, is not about dominating others but about serving and guiding with wisdom and empathy. The idea is to lead without asserting excessive control, recognizing the power of leading by example.

- **Flexibility and adaptability:** The Tao Te Ching emphasizes the importance of flexibility and adaptability in the face of change. Life is portrayed as dynamic, and we are encouraged to embrace change rather than resist it. By being flexible and adaptable, we can navigate the complexities of life more effectively, responding to circumstances with a mind open to transformation.

- **Embracing the mystery:** The Tao Te Ching acknowledges the inherent mystery of existence. It suggests that the ultimate reality is beyond human comprehension and that embracing this mystery is a key to wisdom. The text encourages us to let go of the need for absolute certainty and control, fostering a sense of awe and reverence for the profound mysteries of life.

Tao Te Ching's teachings and principles provide a holistic and timeless guide to living a meaningful and balanced life. The text's enduring relevance lies in its ability to inspire introspection, encourage personal transformation, and offer a profound philosophy for ethical and purposeful living.

Practical Insights For Beginners

For beginners exploring the teachings of the Tao Te Ching, the sometimes abstract nature of the text may seem daunting or even confusing. However, the wisdom within the Tao Te Ching offers practical insights that can be applied to everyday life. Here are some key practical insights to help you as a beginner:

- **Embrace simplicity:** The Tao Te Ching advocates for a simple and uncomplicated way of life. Start by reflecting on areas of your life where you can simplify—whether it be in daily routines, possessions, or relationships. Simplifying allows for a clearer focus on what truly matters and fosters a sense of contentment.

- **Practice mindfulness:** Central to the Taoist philosophy is the idea of being present in the moment. You can incorporate mindfulness practices into your daily life, such as paying full attention to tasks, savoring the taste of food, or being fully engaged in conversations. Mindfulness helps cultivate a deeper connection with the present, fostering a sense of peace and awareness.

- **Cultivate Wu Wei in actions:** Wu Wei encourages us to go with the flow rather than resisting the natural course of events. You can apply this principle by recognizing when to act and when to let things unfold naturally. It involves finding a balance between active engagement and allowing things to happen without unnecessary interference.

- **Seek balance in all things:** Taoism emphasizes the importance of balance in various aspects of life. Start by reflecting on areas where you might be leaning toward extremes and strive to find a middle path. This could involve balancing work and leisure, rest and activity, or even emotional states. Recognizing and addressing imbalances can lead to greater overall well-being.

- **Practice humility:** Humility is a recurring theme in the Tao Te Ching. You can cultivate humility by acknowledging your strengths and weaknesses without ego-driven attachments. Humility fosters openness to learning, the ability to accept feedback, and a greater appreciation for the interconnectedness of all things.

- **Adapt to change:** The Tao Te Ching teaches that change is an inherent part of life, and resisting it can lead to suffering. You can learn to embrace change by cultivating flexibility and adaptability. This involves letting go of rigid expectations and accepting that life is dynamic, filled with ups and downs.

- **Lead by example:** The text offers insights into leadership that can be applied not only in formal leadership roles but also in everyday interactions. Embody leadership qualities by leading with integrity, compassion, and humility. Leadership, according to the Tao Te Ching, is about serving others and setting an example through virtuous actions.

- **Appreciate the journey:** Taoism encourages us to appreciate the journey rather than fixating solely on goals. You can practice this by being present during the process of achieving your aims, finding joy in the steps taken, and understanding that the journey itself holds valuable lessons.

- **Connect with nature:** The Tao Te Ching frequently draws analogies from nature to convey its teachings. Deepen your understanding by spending time in nature, observing its rhythms, and recognizing the harmony that exists in natural processes. This connection to nature can offer a source of inspiration and grounding.

- **Cultivate inner stillness:** In the midst of a busy and often chaotic world, you can benefit from cultivating inner stillness. This involves taking time for meditation, reflection, or any practice that brings a sense of peace and quiet to the mind. Inner stillness allows for better decision-making and a deeper connection with the inner self.

Incorporating these practical insights from the Tao Te Ching into daily life can be a transformative journey. The key is to approach these principles with an open mind, allowing for gradual integration and personal interpretation as one explores the depth of Taoist wisdom.

CHAPTER 5

Wu Wei – Action through Non-Action

We know that Wu Wei is a central concept in Taoist philosophy as presented in the Tao Te Ching. This principle encapsulates a profound understanding of how we can navigate life with a sense of harmony and flow. We have explored the basics of Wu Wei so far, but to grasp the essence correctly, it's crucial to explore its various dimensions and applications more deeply.

At first glance, "non-action" might suggest passivity or doing nothing. However, Wu Wei doesn't advocate for inaction; instead, it emphasizes action that is aligned with the natural course of events. It's about acting without unnecessary effort or resistance, allowing things to unfold organically. It's a state where actions are in tune with the rhythm of the Tao, the underlying principle of the universe.

Of course, the Tao is considered the source and essence of everything, and Wu Wei is the art of aligning yourself with this fundamental force. It involves living in harmony with the natural order of the world, acknowledging that there is a universal flow that, when understood and followed, leads to a more balanced and fulfilling life.

Spontaneity and Intuition

Wu Wei encourages spontaneity in action, trusting our intuition and responding to situations without overthinking. It's about tapping into the innate wisdom that arises when the mind is quiet and receptive. By allowing actions to arise naturally from the present moment, we can navigate life with a sense of grace and ease.

Efficiency and Minimal Effort

In the context of Wu Wei, efficiency is not achieved through force or excessive striving. Instead, it's about finding the most straightforward and effective path. By minimizing unnecessary effort and avoiding the resistance that often accompanies forceful actions, we can accomplish tasks with greater efficiency.

Adapting to Circumstances

Wu Wei acknowledges the ever-changing nature of life. It encourages us to adapt to circumstances rather than rigidly adhering to fixed plans. This adaptability involves being responsive to the ebb and flow of situations, recognizing that resistance to change can lead to frustration and disharmony.

Being Present in the Moment

To practice Wu Wei, we must be fully present in the current moment. Dwelling on the past or anxiously anticipating the future disrupts the natural flow of life. By immersing ourselves in the present, we can respond to the needs of the moment and act in accordance with the unfolding reality.

Letting Go of Control

Wu Wei challenges the notion of absolute control. It suggests that attempting to control every aspect of life is not only futile but can also lead to stress and inner conflict. Letting go of the need for total control allows us to trust the inherent order of the universe and find a more peaceful way of navigating challenges.

Alignment with Personal Nature

Wu Wei extends to the idea of understanding and aligning with our own nature. This involves recognizing our strengths and limitations, embracing authenticity, and acting in a way that is true to our core self. By aligning with our personal nature, we can navigate life with greater integrity and fulfillment.

Applying Wu Wei in Relationships

In interpersonal relationships, Wu Wei encourages a balanced and harmonious approach. It advises against trying to force others to conform to our expectations and instead promotes a more open and accepting attitude.

By allowing relationships to develop naturally, conflicts can be minimized, and connections can deepen authentically.

Cultivating Wu Wei in Daily Life

Practical application of Wu Wei involves integrating its principles into daily activities. It might include finding joy in routine tasks, adapting to unexpected changes with grace, and recognizing when to step back and allow situations to unfold without unnecessary interference.

Overall, Wu Wei is a philosophy that advocates for a way of being that is both active and receptive, purposeful yet flexible. It invites us to dance with the ever-changing rhythm of life, trusting in the inherent wisdom of the Tao. As we deepen our understanding and practice of Wu Wei, we may discover a path to a more harmonious, balanced, and fulfilling existence.

Applying Effortless Action in Daily Life

Applying the principle of effortless action, or Wu Wei, in daily life, involves cultivating a mindset and approach that emphasizes harmony, adaptability, and a natural flow in all activities. Integrating Wu Wei into your daily routine can lead to increased ease, reduced stress, and a more authentic engagement with the present moment.

To help you begin, here a comprehensive exploration of how you can apply the concept of effortless action in various aspects of daily life:

Mindful Awareness:

- **Practice Presence:** Begin by cultivating mindful awareness of the present moment. Be fully engaged in whatever you are doing, whether it's a routine task or a more complex activity.

- **Observe Without Judgment:** Pay attention to your thoughts and actions without immediately judging or reacting. Mindful observation allows for a more considered and intentional response.

Simplicity and Minimalism:

- **Declutter Your Environment:** Simplify your living space by decluttering. A clean and organized environment promotes a sense of calm and reduces mental noise.

- **Streamline Your Schedule:** Avoid overcommitting and streamline your schedule. Prioritize activities that align with your values, allowing you to engage with them more meaningfully.

Efficiency and Focus:

- **Prioritize Tasks:** Identify and prioritize tasks based on their importance. Focus on one task at a time, applying your energy more efficiently without spreading yourself too thin.

- **Flow State:** Cultivate a flow state by immersing yourself fully in an activity. This allows for a natural and effortless progression of actions, often resulting in heightened productivity and satisfaction.

Adaptability and Flexibility:

- **Embrace Change:** Instead of resisting change, embrace it. Recognize that change is a constant in life and practice adaptability in the face of unexpected circumstances.

- **Adjust Expectations:** Be flexible in your expectations. Allow room for deviations from plans and be open to alternative outcomes.

Interpersonal Relationships:

- **Listen Actively:** In conversations, practice active listening. Allow the dialogue to unfold without immediately formulating your response. This creates a space for more meaningful communication.

- **Respond, Don't React:** When faced with conflicts or challenges in relationships, respond thoughtfully instead of reacting impulsively. This measured response aligns with the idea of non-action in Wu Wei.

Work and Creativity:

- **Find Your Flow:** Identify tasks that allow you to enter a state of flow. These are activities that align with your skills and interests, where the boundaries between you and the task seem to disappear.

- **Creative Exploration:** Approach creative endeavors with a sense of exploration rather than rigid goal-setting. Allow the creative process to unfold organically.

Health and Well-being:

- **Holistic Self-Care:** Practice holistic self-care by addressing physical, mental, and emotional well-being. Choose activities and habits that nourish all aspects of your being.

- **Listen to Your Body:** Pay attention to your body's signals. If you feel fatigued or stressed, consider whether you are pushing against the natural flow of your own energy.

Nature Connection:

- **Spend Time in Nature:** Regularly connect with nature. Nature has its own effortless rhythm, and spending time outdoors can help you attune yourself to a more natural and harmonious pace.

- **Observe Natural Patterns:** Learn from the natural world. Observe the cycles, patterns, and interconnectedness found in nature, and reflect on how you can embody these principles in your own life.

Leadership and Decision-Making:

- **Lead by Example:** If you are in a leadership role, lead by example. Demonstrate qualities of humility, adaptability, and ethical decision-making.

- **Decisiveness without Force:** Make decisions decisively but without forcing outcomes. Allow decisions to unfold naturally, and be prepared to adjust course if needed.

Reflection and Self-Inquiry:

- **Regular Reflection:** Set aside time for regular reflection. Assess your actions, intentions, and overall alignment with the principles of Wu Wei.

- **Self-Inquiry:** Engage in self-inquiry to understand your motivations and desires. By understanding yourself better, you can navigate life with greater authenticity.

Applying Wu Wei in daily life is not about relinquishing control or becoming passive. Instead, it is a mindful and intentional approach that encourages alignment with the natural order of things. As you integrate these principles into your daily activities, you may find that a sense of ease, spontaneity, and fulfillment becomes a more integral part of your life journey

Balancing Intention and Spontaneity

Balancing intention and spontaneity is a delicate operation that involves navigating the path between purposeful action and the unexpected surprises life offers. Striking the right equilibrium between these two elements is essential for leading a fulfilling and meaningful life.

Let's explore the interplay of intention and spontaneity, delving into their significance and offering insights on how to maintain a harmonious balance.

Understanding Intention:

1. **Clarity of Purpose:**

- **Setting Goals:** Intention is often associated with setting clear goals. It involves identifying what you want to achieve, creating a roadmap, and aligning your actions with your objectives.

- **Values and Beliefs:** Intentions are closely tied to your values and beliefs. They provide a framework for decision-making and guide your actions in alignment with your core principles.

2. **Focus and Determination:**

- **Channeling Energy:** Intentions provide a focused channel for your energy. They help you direct your efforts toward specific outcomes, preventing dispersion of energy in multiple directions.

- **Overcoming Challenges:** When faced with obstacles, a strong intention can serve as a motivating force, encouraging perseverance and resilience in the pursuit of your goals.

3. **Planning and Strategy:**

- **Strategic Thinking:** Intention involves strategic thinking and planning. It's about considering the steps needed to reach your objectives and anticipating potential challenges along the way.

- **Mindful Decision-Making:** Having clear intentions enables more mindful decision-making. Choices are made with a conscious awareness of how they align with your overall purpose.

Appreciating Spontaneity:

1. **Embracing the Unpredictable:**

- **Creative Potential:** Spontaneity opens the door to creative expression and novel ideas. It allows for unexpected solutions to emerge and fosters a mindset that embraces innovation.

- **Adapting to Change:** Life is inherently unpredictable, and spontaneity enables individuals to adapt to changing circumstances without feeling overwhelmed.

2. **Living in the Present Moment:**

- **Mindfulness:** Spontaneity is closely connected to mindfulness. It involves fully engaging with the present moment, free from excessive planning or preconceived notions.

- **Joy and Playfulness:** Spontaneous actions often bring a sense of joy and playfulness. They allow you to break free from routine and experience the thrill of the unknown.

3. **Building Authentic Connections:**

- **Social Interactions:** Spontaneous moments can lead to more authentic and genuine interactions with others. They create opportunities for shared experiences and deeper connections.

- **Flexibility in Relationships:** Being spontaneous in relationships fosters flexibility and adaptability. It allows for a more dynamic and evolving connection with others.

Balancing the Two:

1. **Flexibility within Structure:**

- **Adapting Plans:** While having clear intentions is important, it's equally crucial to be flexible in adapting plans when unexpected opportunities or challenges arise.

- **Dynamic Goal Setting:** Consider setting goals that allow for flexibility. Instead of rigid outcomes, focus on the essence of what you want to achieve, allowing room for spontaneity in the process.

2. **Cultivating Mindful Awareness:**

- **Present-Moment Awareness:** Develop mindfulness to discern when to stick to your intentions and when to embrace spontaneity. This awareness allows you to navigate situations with a clear understanding of your motives and the unfolding reality.

- **Reflection:** Regularly reflect on your intentions and the role of spontaneity in your life. This self-inquiry helps you refine your goals and assess whether they remain aligned with your evolving values and aspirations.

3. **Embracing the Flow of Life:**

- **The Taoist Perspective:** Drawing from Taoist philosophy, embrace the concept of Wu Wei, or "effortless action." Allow life to unfold naturally, recognizing the balance between guiding your journey with intentions and being open to the organic flow of events.

4. **Practicing Gratitude:**

- **Appreciating Surprises:** Cultivate gratitude for the unexpected gifts and surprises that spontaneity brings. This positive mindset enhances your ability to navigate the uncertainties of life with an open heart.

The Benefits of a Balanced Approach:

It's no surprise that living in balance has many health benefits. Let's look at some of the main ones:

- **Reduced stress and anxiety:** Balancing intention and spontaneity reduces the stress associated with rigid plans. The ability to adapt to unexpected changes fosters a more relaxed and resilient mindset.

- **Enhanced creativity:** Embracing spontaneity injects a sense of freshness and creativity into problem-solving. It encourages thinking outside established frameworks and exploring novel solutions.

- **Deepened relationships:** Spontaneous actions often lead to shared experiences, strengthening bonds in relationships. These shared moments create lasting memories and contribute to the depth of connections.

- **Personal growth:** A balanced approach fosters adaptability, a key component of personal growth. It encourages learning from unexpected situations and leveraging them as opportunities for development.

Challenges and Considerations:

Nothing is without its challenges and approaching this element of Taoism can be difficult at the start. The main challenges most beginners face are:

- **Overemphasis on control:** Individuals who lean heavily toward intention may struggle with letting go of control. Recognizing the limits of control and embracing the unknown can be challenging but is essential for a balanced approach.

- **Fear of uncertainty:** A fear of uncertainty can hinder spontaneity. Building resilience and cultivating a positive mindset can help overcome this fear and foster a more open approach to the unknown.

Balancing intention and spontaneity is not about choosing one over the other but about integrating both seamlessly into your approach to life. It involves navigating the complexities of goal-setting and planning while remaining open to the surprises and opportunities that arise in each moment.

By cultivating this balance, you embark on a journey that is purposeful, dynamic, and rich with the potential for growth and fulfillment.

CHAPTER 6

Inner Alchemy – Cultivating
Inner Energy

M editation and inner practices are integral components of Taoist philosophy, offering a means to cultivate inner peace, harmony, and a deeper connection with the Tao. Rooted in ancient Chinese wisdom, Taoist meditation emphasizes the alignment of body, mind, and spirit, fostering a state of balance and tranquility.

In this chapter, let's delve into the foundations, principles, and key practices of Taoist meditation and inner cultivation.

Foundations of Taoist Meditation

We know that Taoism, as a philosophical and spiritual tradition, centers around the concept of the Tao—the source, essence, and natural order of the universe. Taoist meditation seeks to align individuals with the flow of the Tao, allowing them to experience inner harmony.

Also central to Taoist meditation is the principle of Wu Wei. It involves cultivating a state of relaxed awareness where one allows the natural flow of life to unfold without unnecessary resistance. Mindfulness and meditation allow this to happen more easily.

Taoism recognizes the interplay of Yin and Yang, opposing yet complementary forces. Taoist meditation aims to balance these energies within the body and mind, promoting overall harmony.

Principles of Taoist Meditation:

Taoist meditation is no different to any other type of meditation you would do, and it aims to bring you closer to the Tao. Here are some common methods:

- **Mindfulness awareness and present moment focus:** Taoist meditation encourages mindful awareness of the present moment. Through this, we learn to observe our thoughts without attachment, cultivating a state of non-judgmental awareness.

- **Breath awareness:** Conscious breathing is a cornerstone of Taoist meditation. Emphasizing natural and relaxed breathing, we can focus on our breath to anchor our awareness and promote a sense of calm.

- **Cultivating inner energy:** Taoist meditation incorporates the concept of "nei dan" or inner alchemy. Through visualization, breath control, and focused awareness, we aim to refine and circulate the body's vital energy (Qi) to promote physical and spiritual well-being.

- **Nature as a Mirror:** Taoist meditation often draws inspiration from nature. Through this, we seek to align ourselves with the natural rhythms of the world, using the elements and natural imagery to deepen our connection with the Tao.

Key Practices of Taoist Meditation

- **Zhan Zhuang (Standing Like a Tree) - Rooting and Grounding:** This foundational practice involves standing in a relaxed yet alert posture, connecting with the earth's energy. Zhan Zhuang aims to build strength, stability, and a sense of rootedness.

- **Dao Yin - Gentle Movements:** Dao Yin exercises are gentle movements that promote the flow of Qi. These exercises, often resembling flowing and harmonious stretches, aim to balance energy and enhance flexibility.

- **Nei Gong (Internal Skill) - Breath Work and Visualization:** Nei Gong incorporates breath work, visualization, and specific movements to cultivate and direct the internal energy. It is a comprehensive system of internal practices within Taoist meditation.

- **Tai Chi and Qi Gong - Flowing Movements:** Tai Chi and Qi Gong, though also considered martial arts, are deeply rooted in Taoist principles. The flowing, slow movements help harmonize body, mind, and breath, promoting balance and flexibility.

- **Reflection and Self-Inquiry:** Taoist meditation extends beyond physical practices to include contemplative exercises. Followers may engage in reflective practices and self-inquiry to deepen their understanding of the Tao and their own nature.

- **Mindful Living:** Taoist meditation is not confined to formal practice sessions. Through this, we aim to bring the principles of mindfulness, balance, and Wu Wei into our everyday activities, fostering a seamless integration of meditation into daily life.

- **Compassion and Humility:** Taoist meditation seeks not only personal well-being but also the cultivation of virtues such as compassion, humility, and kindness. These qualities are seen as essential for harmonious living and spiritual development.

Challenges and Considerations

Most people try meditation once and give up. This is because it doesn't come without its challenges. However, learning to be patient and overcome these issues will help you to reap the benefits within a short amount of time.

Most people new to Taoist practices, and indeed meditation itself, struggle with patience and consistency. After all, it is a long-term commitment. It is a journey that unfolds gradually, and we are encouraged to approach it with dedication.

It's also wise to take guidance from other people around you. Traditionally, Taoist meditation was transmitted from master to disciple. While self-practice is valuable, guidance from an experienced teacher can provide insights and corrections that enhance the depth of the practice.

Exploring The Concept of Qi (Chi) Energy

Qi, also spelled as Chi, is a fundamental concept in traditional Chinese philosophy, particularly within Taoism and Traditional Chinese Medicine (TCM). It is a multifaceted concept that encompasses the vital life force or energy that permeates the universe, animates living beings, and maintains the balance of opposing forces.

Let's delve into the concept of Qi, examining its various aspects, its significance in different contexts, and its practical applications.

First things first, what is Qi?

Qi is often described as the vital energy or life force that flows through all living things and the cosmos. It is an invisible and pervasive force that is both within and around us.

Qi is dynamic, ever-changing, and in constant motion. It is the underlying principle that governs the cyclical processes of nature and life.

In the context of Yin and Yang, Qi is understood as having both Yin and Yang aspects. It represents the interplay and balance of these opposing forces, embodying the principle of dynamic equilibrium. The harmony of Yin and Yang within the body and the natural world is essential for the free flow of Qi and the maintenance of health.

Traditional Chinese Medicine posits that Qi circulates along specific pathways called meridians or channels. There are twelve main meridians, each associated with a different organ system. The smooth and balanced flow of Qi through these meridians is crucial for maintaining health. When Qi becomes stagnant or imbalanced, it can lead to physical or emotional disturbances.

Types and Functions of Qi

Original Qi (Yuan Qi):

- **Essence of Life:** Yuan Qi is considered the foundational energy that a person inherits at birth. It is associated with genetics, prenatal influences, and constitutional factors.

- **Determines Vitality:** The state of Yuan Qi is believed to determine a person's vitality, resilience, and overall life potential.

Nutritive Qi (Ying Qi):

- **Nourishing the Body:** Ying Qi is responsible for nourishing the body. It circulates through the meridians and transports nutrients to various organs and tissues.

- **Linked to Blood:** Ying Qi is closely associated with blood, and its proper circulation is essential for maintaining health and vitality.

Defensive Qi (Wei Qi):

- **Immune Function:** Wei Qi is the body's defensive energy, providing protection against external pathogens. It forms a protective layer beneath the skin and helps regulate the body's immune response.

- **External Influences:** Wei Qi plays a crucial role in resisting external factors that may cause illness or imbalance.

Qi in Martial Arts

Internal martial arts, such as Tai Chi and Baguazhang, emphasize the cultivation and expression of Qi for martial purposes. Followers learn to move with a relaxed and connected energy, harnessing the power of Qi in their movements.

However, Qi in martial arts is not merely physical energy but involves the integration of mental focus and intent. Followers aim to cultivate a state of internal stillness while maintaining alertness and responsiveness.

Qi in Acupuncture

Acupuncture, a key component of Traditional Chinese Medicine, involves the insertion of thin needles into specific points along the meridians to regulate and balance the flow of Qi. The goal is to restore harmony by addressing imbalances in the circulation of Qi, which is believed to be linked to various health conditions.

Qi, as a concept, is expansive and multifaceted, with implications ranging from physical health and martial arts to meditation and spiritual cultivation. It reflects a holistic understanding of the interconnectedness of the body, mind, and the broader universe within various Chinese traditions.

Whether explored through the lens of Traditional Chinese Medicine, martial arts, or Taoist philosophy, the concept of Qi invites us to cultivate a harmonious relationship with the vital energy that animates and sustains life.

Techniques for Cultivating and Balancing Inner Energy

Cultivating and balancing inner energy is a central focus in various spiritual and traditional practices, including Taoist philosophy, Yoga, and Traditional Chinese Medicine (TCM). In this section, let's explore the diverse techniques used across different traditions to cultivate and balance inner energy...

Breath Control and Pranayama

Deep and conscious breathing is a fundamental technique to cultivate inner energy. It involves inhaling slowly, deeply, and fully, allowing the breath to reach the lower abdomen, and exhaling completely. Deep breathing activates the parasympathetic nervous system, promoting relaxation and reducing stress. This, in turn, supports the free flow of inner energy.

Pranayama Techniques:

- **Alternate Nostril Breathing (Nadi Shodhana):** This technique involves breathing through alternate nostrils, balancing the flow of energy in the body.

- **Ujjayi Breathing:** Also known as "ocean breath," Ujjayi involves breathing with a slight constriction at the back of the throat, producing a soft sound. It is believed to enhance concentration and inner energy.

Meditation and Mindfulness Practices

- **Breath Awareness Meditation:** Many meditation practices focus on observing the breath. By bringing attention to the breath, we cultivate mindfulness and create a foundation for inner energy to flow smoothly.

- **Mantra Meditation:** Repeating a mantra or sacred sound can help concentrate the mind and channel inner energy toward a specific intention or purpose.

Mindful Movement Practices:

- **Tai Chi and Qi Gong:** These Chinese martial arts involve slow, deliberate movements coordinated with breath control. The practices aim to cultivate and balance Qi, promoting a harmonious flow of inner energy.

- **Yoga Asanas:** Yoga postures, when combined with breath awareness, help release blockages and tension in the body, facilitating the circulation of Prana.

Visualization and Inner Alchemy

- **Microcosmic Orbit Meditation:** In Taoist practices, the Microcosmic Orbit involves visualizing the circulation of Qi along the meridians, forming a loop between the Ren and Du channels. This meditation aims to balance and refine inner energy.

- **Dantian Cultivation:** Focusing on the three Dantian points (energy centers) in the body, particularly the lower Dantian located in the abdomen, helps accumulate and store Qi.

Chakra Meditation

- **Chakra Visualization:** In Yogic traditions, chakras are considered energy centers along the spine. Meditation involves visualizing and balancing the energy flow through these chakras, promoting harmony in the body and mind.

Sound and Vibrational Practices

- **Tuning Forks and Singing Bowls:** The vibrational frequencies produced by tuning forks or singing bowls are believed to influence the body's energy. Sound healing practices can help release energetic blockages and restore balance.

- **Mantras and Chanting:** The repetition of sacred sounds or chants creates vibrations that resonate with specific energies, fostering a harmonious balance of inner energy.

Acupressure and Energy Work

- **Stimulating Energy Points:** Acupressure involves applying pressure to specific points along the body's meridians. By stimulating these points, practitioners aim to release blocked energy and restore balance.

- **Reflexology:** Focused on the feet, hands, or ears, reflexology stimulates specific reflex points to promote energy flow throughout the body.

Reiki and Energy Healing

- **Channeling Universal Energy:** In practices like Reiki, practitioners channel universal energy to the recipient, promoting relaxation, healing, and balance. This involves the transfer of subtle energy through the hands.

Diet and Lifestyle Practices

- **Qi-Nourishing Foods:** Traditional Chinese Medicine emphasizes the importance of a balanced diet to support the circulation of Qi. Foods like dark leafy greens, root vegetables, and whole grains are considered nourishing for Qi.

- **Hydration:** Proper hydration is essential for the smooth flow of inner energy. Water helps lubricate joints, flush out toxins, and support overall vitality.

Mindful Movement in Daily Life

- **Walking Meditation:** Integrating mindfulness into daily activities, such as walking, helps maintain a continuous flow of energy. Walking mindfully involves being present with each step and breath.

- **Postural Awareness:** Maintaining good posture throughout the day is crucial for preventing blockages in the flow of energy. Mindful awareness of body alignment contributes to overall well-being.

Nature Connection

- **Shinrin-Yoku (Forest Bathing):** Spending time in nature, particularly in forests, is believed to enhance the connection with natural energy. Forest bathing involves immersing yourself in the sights, sounds, and smells of the forest to promote well-being.

- **Grounding Practices:** Walking barefoot on natural surfaces, known as grounding or earthing, allows the body to connect with the earth's energy, promoting a sense of balance.

Qi-Enhancing Herbs and Supplements

- **Adaptogenic Herbs:** Herbs like ginseng, astragalus, and ashwagandha are considered adaptogens that support the body's ability to adapt to stressors, enhance vitality, and promote balanced energy.

- **Qi-Tonifying Formulas:** Traditional Chinese Medicine formulations often include herbs to tonify Qi. These may be prescribed based on an individual's specific imbalances.

Cultivating and balancing inner energy involves a holistic approach that integrates physical, mental, and spiritual practices. By exploring and incorporating these diverse techniques, we can create a harmonious environment for the free flow of vital life force. Whether drawn from ancient traditions or modern approaches, these practices empower us to deepen our connection with inner energy, fostering a sense of balance, vitality, and well-being.

CHAPTER 7

Taoist Ethics and Virtues

We've covered the primary ethics that bring together the Taoist philosophy, but there is more to learn. In this chapter, we'll cover some of the other ethics and virtues, such as living naturally, embracing compassion, and understanding simplicity.

Ziran (Naturalness)

Ziran refers to living in accordance with one's true nature and the natural order of the world. It involves embracing simplicity, spontaneity, and authenticity. By embodying the principle of Ziran, we learn to adapt to circumstances gracefully, accepting the ebb and flow of life without undue attachment or resistance.

Virtue and Compassion

De, often translated as virtue or integrity, is a central concept in Taoist morality. Cultivating virtue involves aligning one's actions with the principles of the Tao, fostering qualities such as humility, compassion, and sincerity.

Taoist sages advocate leading by example rather than imposing moral principles on others. Through embodying virtue, we inspire those around us to follow a similar path.

Compassion and Wu Ren (Non-contention)

Taoism places a strong emphasis on compassion and benevolence. Wu Ren, or non-contention, involves avoiding unnecessary conflict and treating others with kindness.

Through this, followers are encouraged to alleviate suffering in the world by practicing compassion and understanding. By avoiding contention, we contribute to the overall harmony of the community.

Simplicity (Pu) and Humility

The concept of Pu encourages us to embrace simplicity in our lifestyles. This involves reducing desires, materialism, and unnecessary complexities. By simplifying life and finding contentment in the present moment, we cultivate inner peace and harmony.

Humility

Humility in Taoism is characterized by a willingness to yield, be flexible, and acknowledge the interconnectedness of all things. It involves recognizing our place within the larger cosmic order.

Moderation (Zho) and Balance

Zho, or moderation, advocates avoiding extremes and finding balance in all aspects of life. This principle aligns with the natural rhythms of the Tao. Taoism teaches that excessive behavior, whether in pursuit of wealth, pleasure, or power, disrupts our harmony and the larger community.

Spontaneity and Simplicity (P'u)

P'u, or simplicity, is associated with naturalness and spontaneity. Taoist sages advise against forced or contrived actions and instead advocate for actions that arise spontaneously. By simplifying life and embracing spontaneity, we align ourselves with the natural order and experience a sense of ease and effortlessness.

Non-attachment and Detachment (Wu You)

Wu You emphasizes non-attachment to desires and outcomes. Taoist morality teaches that excessive attachment leads to suffering and disrupts the natural flow of life. By letting go of attachment to future outcomes, we find contentment in the present moment, appreciating life as it unfolds.

Ziran (Self-so)

Ziran, often translated as self-so or spontaneity, involves acting in accordance with our true nature. This principle encourages us to detach from societal expectations and external influences.

By being self-so, we can express their authentic selves without conforming to external pressures, fostering a sense of inner freedom and harmony.

Taoist moral principles are deeply embedded in Chinese culture and philosophy. Individual interpretations may vary based on cultural backgrounds, personal beliefs, and philosophical perspectives. Applying Taoist moral principles in everyday life requires a balance between ideals and practical considerations. Followers may face challenges in aligning completely with these principles in a complex and fast-paced world.

However, the moral principles of Taoism provides a flexible guide for those seeking to live in harmony with themselves, others, and the natural world. By cultivating virtue, embracing simplicity, and finding balance, followers of Taoism aim to navigate life with authenticity and wisdom. These principles continue to inspire us on a timeless journey toward inner harmony and a harmonious relationship with the Tao.

Embracing Simplicity, Compassion, and Humility

Embracing simplicity, compassion, and humility forms a profound cornerstone of various spiritual and philosophical traditions, with each principle contributing to a balanced and meaningful way of life.

This triad of values, often interwoven in the fabric of ethical teachings, transcends cultural and religious boundaries, promoting a universal approach to fostering personal growth and harmonious relationships with others and the world.

Let's explore each of these principles in-depth...

Embracing Simplicity

Simplicity involves paring down the complexities of life, minimizing unnecessary material possessions, and simplifying daily routines. Embracing simplicity means finding contentment in the present moment rather than constantly pursuing material accumulation. It involves appreciating life's essentials and reducing dependence on external sources of validation.

Cultivating Inner Peace

Simplifying life leads to mindful living, where we are fully present and engaged in each moment. This mindfulness contributes to inner peace and a sense of tranquility.

A simple and uncluttered lifestyle extends to mental and emotional realms, promoting mental clarity and reducing the mental burden of excessive desires and attachments.

Environmental Consciousness

Simplicity aligns with environmental consciousness by promoting sustainable practices. Choosing a minimalist and eco-friendly lifestyle contributes to the well-being of the planet.

By being mindful of consumption, we embrace simplicity and play a role in reducing our environmental footprint and fostering a more sustainable future.

Practicing Compassion

Compassion involves the ability to connect with others on a deep emotional level, understanding their joys, sorrows, and struggles. It means recognizing the shared human experience, fostering empathy, and cultivating a sense of interconnectedness.

Alleviating Suffering

Compassion translates into concrete actions aimed at alleviating the suffering of others. Small acts of kindness, empathy, and support contribute to creating a more compassionate world. Additionally, compassion involves actively listening to others without judgment, providing a safe space for them to express themselves and feel understood.

Self-Compassion

Remember, embracing compassion extends to ourselves too. Self-compassion involves treating yourself with the same kindness and understanding offered to others, fostering resilience and self-love.

Ultimately, compassion doesn't mean sacrificing personal well-being. It involves setting healthy boundaries while still contributing positively to the lives of others.

Cultivating Humility

Humility stems from recognizing the interdependence of all living beings. It involves understanding that every individual is part of a larger whole, and no one is above or below another. Humility fosters an appreciation for the diversity of experiences and perspectives, acknowledging that each person has a unique contribution to make.

Learning from Others

Humility involves a willingness to learn from others, regardless of their background or status. It acknowledges that everyone has valuable insights and experiences to share. Embracing humility means viewing challenges as opportunities for growth and learning. It involves acknowledging that there is always room for improvement.

Service to Others

Humility manifests in selfless service to others. It involves contributing without seeking personal recognition or validation. Humble leaders inspire through their actions rather than imposing authority. They lead by example, demonstrating the strength that comes from humility.

Balancing Simplicity, Compassion, and Humility

Embracing simplicity, compassion, and humility involves integrating these principles into a holistic approach to life. Rather than viewing them as isolated virtues, we must strive to embody them collectively.

Simplicity supports compassion by reducing distractions, allowing us to focus on meaningful connections. Humility reinforces simplicity by recognizing the modesty and interconnectedness of all life.

- **Mindful Decision-Making:** The triad of simplicity, compassion, and humility guides mindful decision-making. Through this, we consider the impact of our choices on ourselves, others, and the environment, promoting a responsible and ethical lifestyle.

- **Prioritizing Relationships:** These principles prioritize meaningful connections over material pursuits, fostering deep and authentic relationships.

- **Cultivating a Virtuous Character:** Embracing simplicity, compassion, and humility contributes to the cultivation of a virtuous character. We must strive to live authentically, with integrity, kindness, and a sense of interconnectedness.

- **Inner Transformation:** Practicing these principles leads to inner transformation, fostering a sense of purpose, joy, and fulfillment that extends beyond external circumstances.

Embracing simplicity, compassion, and humility offers a transformative pathway to a more meaningful and interconnected existence. As we integrate these principles into our daily lives, we contribute not only to personal well-being but also to the creation of a more compassionate, sustainable, and harmonious world.

By nurturing simplicity in the way we live, showing compassion to others and ourselves, and embracing humility in our interactions, we can collectively foster a positive ripple effect that extends far beyond individual lives.

Ethical Guidelines For a Harmonious Life

Ethical guidelines provide a moral compass, guiding us toward actions that promote personal well-being, positive relationships, and a balanced connection with the world. These guidelines often draw inspiration from various cultural, philosophical, and spiritual traditions, offering principles that transcend boundaries and contribute to the creation of a harmonious and flourishing existence.

Let's explore the ethical guidelines that can contribute to a harmonious life...

Honesty and Truthfulness

Cultivate a commitment to honesty and transparency in all interactions. Be truthful in your words and actions, fostering trust in relationships. Uphold personal integrity by aligning your actions with your values. Make choices that resonate with your sense of virtue.

Compassion and Empathy

Practice empathy by seeking to understand the perspectives and feelings of others. Compassion involves a genuine concern for the well-being of all beings.

Remember to engage in acts of kindness, both big and small, to contribute positively to the lives of those around you.

Practice Mindfulness and Presence

Cultivate mindfulness by being fully present in each moment. Mindful living promotes a deeper connection with oneself and the surrounding environment. Minimize distractions and practice focus to enhance the quality of your interactions and experiences.

Gratitude

Develop a sense of gratitude for the simple joys of life. Acknowledge and appreciate the positive aspects of your experiences, fostering contentment. Also express gratitude to others for their contributions and support, strengthening interpersonal relationships.

Promote Harmony in Relationships

Foster harmonious relationships by practicing active listening. Give others your full attention and seek to understand their perspectives before responding. Always communicate openly and honestly, expressing your thoughts and feelings clearly, while maintaining respect for others.

Forgiveness and Letting Go

Embrace forgiveness as a means to release resentment and foster emotional healing. Letting go of grudges contributes to inner peace and harmonious relationships. Reflect on your own actions and cultivate a willingness to forgive yourself, acknowledging that everyone is on a journey of growth.

Live with Simplicity and Moderation

Embrace simplicity by reducing reliance on material possessions for happiness. Contentment arises from appreciating the present moment rather than constantly seeking external validation.

It's important to practice moderation in all aspects of life, including consumption of resources, food, and entertainment. Strive for a balanced and sustainable lifestyle.

Environmental Stewardship

Make environmentally conscious choices to contribute to the well-being of the planet. Always consider the ecological impact of your actions and seek sustainable alternatives.

Develop a sense of respect and awe for the natural world. Connect with nature to foster a deeper understanding of the interconnectedness of all life.

Cultivate Inner Peace and Self-Reflection

Cultivate inner peace through practices such as meditation and contemplation. These practices promote self-awareness and emotional balance. Engage in mind-body practices like yoga or Tai Chi to harmonize the physical and mental aspects of your being. These practices contribute to a sense of inner balance.

Self-Reflection and Self-Improvement

Take time for regular self-reflection to assess your actions, values, and goals. Use self-awareness as a tool for personal growth and improvement. Foster a mindset of continuous learning and self-improvement. Embrace challenges as opportunities for growth and development.

Act with Compassion Towards All Beings

Extend compassion to all living beings, including animals. Practice kindness by considering the well-being of animals in your choices and actions. Avoid causing harm to sentient beings and strive to live in harmony with the entire web of life.

Social Responsibility

Engage in activities that contribute positively to your community. Social responsibility involves recognizing the interconnectedness of society and taking action to enhance the well-being of all.

Advocate for justice and equality, working towards creating a society where everyone has the opportunity to thrive.

Cultivate Humility and Open-mindedness

Cultivate humility by recognizing the value of diverse perspectives and experiences. Embrace opportunities to learn from people with different backgrounds. Challenge and eradicate prejudiced beliefs, and approach others with an open heart and mind, fostering understanding and acceptance.

Service to Others

Cultivate humility through selfless service to others. Engage in acts of kindness without expecting personal gain, contributing to the well-being of the broader community.

Always recognize the strengths and contributions of others, fostering a collaborative spirit. Humility involves acknowledging that collective efforts often lead to greater success.

These guidelines serve as a compass, guiding us on a path toward personal growth, interpersonal harmony, and a positive impact on the world.

CHAPTER 8

Taoism and Nature

D eveloping a deeper connection with nature is an essential and transformative journey that we can embark upon to enhance our well-being and cultivate a greater sense of harmony with the world around us. In today's fast-paced and technologically-driven society, we often find ourselves disconnected from the natural world, leading to various physical, mental, and emotional imbalances. Therefore, fostering a deeper connection with nature can offer numerous benefits for both us and the planet.

One simple way to deepen this connection is by spending more time outdoors. Whether it's a stroll through a nearby park, a hike in the mountains, or a quiet moment by the ocean, immersing yourself in natural environments can be profoundly rejuvenating. Nature has the power to inspire awe and wonder, encouraging a sense of humility and interconnectedness with the larger ecosystem.

Additionally, observing the intricate patterns of a flower, the rhythmic flow of a river, or the gentle rustling of leaves in the wind can bring a heightened awareness of the beauty and complexity of the natural world.

Practicing mindfulness in nature is another powerful way to strengthen our bond with the environment. Mindfulness involves being fully present in the moment, paying attention to our thoughts and feelings without judgment. When applied to nature, this practice can deepen the sensory experience, allowing us to truly engage with our surroundings. The rustling of leaves, the scent of pine, and the warmth of sunlight on our skin become anchors that root us in the present moment, fostering a profound connection with the environment.

Cultivating a sense of environmental stewardship is also crucial. Understanding the interdependence of all living beings and recognizing the impact of human activities on the planet can motivate us to adopt more sustainable and eco-friendly lifestyles. Simple actions such as reducing waste, conserving energy, and supporting environmental initiatives contribute to the well-being of the earth and reinforce the sense of responsibility toward the natural world.

Incorporating nature into daily routines, such as gardening, birdwatching, or simply taking breaks outdoors, can have a positive impact on mental health. Research suggests that exposure to nature can reduce stress, anxiety, and depression while promoting overall psychological well-being. The therapeutic effect of nature is so profound that it has given rise to practices like ecotherapy, where individuals engage in outdoor activities as part of their mental health treatment.

Ultimately, deepening our connection with nature is not just a personal endeavor; it is a collective responsibility. As more of us recognize the intrinsic value of nature, there is an increased likelihood of fostering a global mindset that prioritizes environmental conservation and sustainable living. In this way, a deepening connection with nature becomes a transformative force, shaping not only individual well-being but also contributing to the preservation of the planet for future generations.

Eco-spirituality in Taoist Philosophy

Eco-spirituality is a profound and harmonious approach to the interconnectedness between humanity and the natural world. Within Taoist philosophy, eco-spirituality involves recognizing and aligning oneself with the natural order of the universe, fostering a deep sense of reverence for the environment, and understanding the interdependence of all things.

Of course, central to Taoist eco-spirituality is the idea of Wu Wei, often translated as "non-action" or "effortless action." Wu Wei does not advocate for passivity but encourages us to act in harmony with the natural flow of events. In the context of eco-spirituality, it suggests that we should not impose our will upon nature but rather observe and adapt to the rhythms and patterns of the natural world. This approach encourages a profound respect for the environment and acknowledges that interfering with the delicate balance of nature can have profound consequences.

The Tao Te Ching offers insights into eco-spirituality. Verses within the Tao Te Ching speak of the Tao as the source of all things, emphasizing the interconnectedness and cyclical nature of existence. The text encourages us to embrace simplicity, humility, and a deep understanding of the natural order to live in harmony with the Tao.

Taoist eco-spirituality is also closely tied to the concept of Yin and Yang, representing the dualistic nature of existence. These opposing forces are not in opposition but rather complementary and interdependent. In the realm of eco-spirituality, this concept underscores the dynamic equilibrium in nature, where opposing forces, such as growth and decay, are integral parts of a larger, harmonious whole.

Nature is considered a sacred manifestation of the Tao in Taoist philosophy. The mountains, rivers, plants, and animals are not merely resources for human use but expressions of the divine. This perspective fosters a deep sense of gratitude and responsibility toward the natural world. Practitioners of Taoist eco-spirituality seek to cultivate a mindful awareness of the environment and strive to live in a way that minimizes harm to the earth.

Taoist rituals and practices often involve ceremonies that honor nature and express gratitude for the gifts it provides. These rituals may include offerings, meditation in natural settings, and symbolic acts that emphasize the interconnectedness of all living things. Through these practices, we can aim to attune ourselves to the rhythms of the natural world and cultivate a spiritual connection with the earth.

In essence, Taoist eco-spirituality encourages us to transcend the human-centered perspective and recognize ourselves as integral parts of a vast and interconnected web of life. By embracing the principles of Wu Wei, Yin and Yang, and the sacredness of nature, Taoist philosophy offers a holistic and spiritually enriching approach to living in harmony with the earth.

Practices for Aligning With the Natural World

Various practices can help us deepen our connection to the natural world, fostering a sense of well-being and ecological mindfulness. To help you out, here are some practices for aligning with the natural world:

- **Nature Meditation:** Engage in meditation outdoors, whether it's in a park, garden, or by a body of water. Sit quietly, focus on your breath, and observe the sounds, scents, and sensations around you. This practice enhances mindfulness and helps attune your awareness to the present moment in nature.

- **Nature Walks and Hikes:** Take regular walks or hikes in natural settings. Whether it's a forest trail, a beach, or a mountain path, spending time in nature allows you to immerse yourself in the surroundings, observe the natural beauty, and feel a sense of connection with the earth.

- **Nature Journaling:** Keep a nature journal to document your observations and experiences in natural settings. Record the sights, sounds, and feelings you encounter. Over time, this practice can deepen your connection as you become more attuned to the subtle changes and cycles in the environment.

- **Seasonal Celebrations:** Acknowledge and celebrate the changing seasons. Engage in rituals or simple ceremonies during solstices, equinoxes, and other natural milestones. This practice helps align your life with the cyclical patterns of nature, fostering a deeper appreciation for its inherent rhythms.

- **Sustainable Living Practices:** Adopt sustainable habits that reduce your ecological footprint. This includes recycling, conserving energy, reducing waste, and choosing eco-friendly products. By living in harmony with the earth's resources, you align your lifestyle with the principles of environmental stewardship.

- **Mindful Gardening:** If possible, cultivate a garden or tend to indoor plants. Gardening fosters a direct connection with the soil and the cycles of growth. Practicing mindfulness while gardening allows you to appreciate the interconnectedness of all living things.

- **Stargazing and Moon Watching:** Spend time observing the night sky. Whether it's stargazing or moon watching, connecting with celestial rhythms can provide a sense of awe and remind you of the vastness of the natural world.

- **Silent Contemplation:** Dedicate moments of silent contemplation in natural settings. Sit quietly and listen to the sounds of nature, observe the movement of the wind, or feel the warmth of the sun. This silent communion with the environment fosters a sense of peace and interconnectedness.

- **Primitive Skills and Crafts:** Learn primitive skills or traditional crafts that connect you with nature, such as fire-making, shelter-building, or natural crafts. These activities not only deepen your understanding of the environment but also foster a sense of self-sufficiency.

- **Animal Observation:** Take time to observe and appreciate wildlife. Whether it's birdwatching, observing insects, or studying the behavior of animals, this practice enhances your awareness of the diversity of life and your place within the ecosystem.

These practices, when integrated into daily life, contribute to a richer connection with the natural world. By aligning with the earth's rhythms, we can cultivate a greater sense of purpose and general well-being.

CHAPTER 9

Rituals and Symbols in Taoism

R ituals and ceremonies play a significant role in the practice of Taoism. Rooted in the idea of living in harmony with the Tao, or the Way, Taoist rituals aim to align followers with the natural order and establish a connection with the divine forces that govern the universe.

Let's explore some of the key aspects of Taoist rituals and ceremonies...

Altars and Sacred Spaces

Taoist rituals often take place at home or in Taoist temples where followers create altars and sacred spaces. These spaces are adorned with symbolic objects, incense, and images of Taoist deities. The arrangement of these items is carefully considered to represent the balance and harmony inherent in Taoist philosophy.

Offerings and Ritual Objects

Offerings are an essential part of Taoist ceremonies. These can include fruits, vegetables, rice, tea, and other items, symbolizing abundance and respect for the gifts of the Earth. Ritual objects like candles, incense, and ceremonial implements are used to invoke spiritual energies and create a sacred atmosphere.

Taoist Festivals

Taoist festivals are occasions for elaborate rituals and celebrations. The most significant of these is the Qingming Festival, also known as the Tomb-Sweeping Day, during which families honor their ancestors. Other festivals include the Taoist New Year and the birthday celebrations of Taoist deities. These festivals involve processions, ceremonies, and community gatherings.

Divination Practices

Taoists often use divination practices to seek guidance from the spiritual realm. Techniques such as casting lots, consulting the I Ching (Book of Changes), or observing natural phenomena are employed to gain insights into the unfolding of events and to make decisions in accordance with the Tao.

Taoist Meditation

While not always considered a formal ritual, Taoist meditation is a crucial aspect of Taoist practice. Meditation is used to still the mind, cultivate inner peace, and align oneself with the Tao. Some Taoist meditation techniques involve breath control, visualization, and the circulation of internal energy (Qi).

Taoist Martial Arts and Ritual Movements

Certain forms of Taoist martial arts, such as Tai Chi and Qigong, are considered ritualistic practices. These movements are designed not only for physical health but also for cultivating spiritual energy and balance. Followers often incorporate slow, deliberate motions and breathing exercises into these rituals.

Taoist Alchemy

Taoist alchemy is a spiritual practice aimed at achieving immortality and spiritual enlightenment. The alchemical process involves inner transformations through meditation, breath control, and visualization. Followers seek to harmonize the dualistic elements within themselves and attain a state of oneness with the Tao.

Taoist Priesthood

Taoist rituals are often officiated by Taoist priests or priestesses who have undergone specific training and initiation. These individuals serve as intermediaries between the human realm and the divine, guiding the community in spiritual practices, performing rituals, and offering blessings.

Purification Rites

Purification is a common theme in Taoist rituals, symbolizing the removal of impurities and obstacles on both a physical and spiritual level. Water, incense, and chanting are often used in purification rites to cleanse the ritual space and participants.

Taoist rituals and ceremonies vary across different sects and traditions within Taoism. However, they share a common thread of seeking harmony with the Tao and acknowledging the interconnectedness of the spiritual and natural realms. Through these rituals, Taoists aim to cultivate a balanced and enlightened way of life in accordance with the principles of the Tao.

Understanding Symbolic Elements

Understanding symbolic elements is a key aspect of decoding meaning in various cultural, religious, and artistic contexts. Symbols serve as powerful communicators, transcending language barriers and conveying complex concepts with a single image, word, or gesture.

Symbols are deeply ingrained in cultural contexts, representing shared values, beliefs, and traditions. Understanding cultural symbols is essential for appreciating the nuances of different societies. For example, the lotus flower symbolizes purity and enlightenment in various Eastern cultures, while the eagle may represent freedom and strength in Western cultures.

Religions often employ symbols to convey profound spiritual truths and connect believers with the divine. Crosses, crescent moons, mandalas, and many other religious symbols carry layers of significance and serve as focal points for worship. Interpretation of these symbols often requires knowledge of religious teachings and traditions.

Artists also use symbols to convey deeper meanings in their work. Colors, shapes, and objects can be loaded with symbolism, adding complexity to visual and literary art. For instance, the use of a red rose in literature may symbolize love, while a broken chain in a painting might represent liberation.

Certain symbols tap into archetypal themes that resonate across cultures and time periods. Carl Jung, a Swiss psychiatrist, introduced the concept of archetypes and argued that symbols such as the hero, the mother, and the serpent have universal significance. Understanding these archetypal symbols can provide insight into collective human experiences.

Of course, flags, anthems, and national emblems are powerful symbols that represent the identity and values of a nation. Understanding these symbols is crucial for comprehending the cultural and historical context of a country. For example, the bald eagle in the United States is a symbol of freedom and strength.

Rituals and ceremonies often involve symbolic elements that carry specific meanings within a given cultural or religious tradition. These symbols may include gestures, attire, objects, and actions that convey participants' connection to the sacred and the spiritual.

We can also look at logos and brand symbols which are integral to corporate identity and marketing. These symbols are carefully designed to convey the values, mission, and identity of a company. Understanding corporate symbols is essential for consumers to interpret the intended message and associations.

Alphabets and writing systems are themselves symbolic elements, representing sounds, words, and meanings. Understanding written symbols is fundamental to effective communication and literacy. Different scripts around the world carry cultural and historical significance.

As individuals, we may adopt personal symbols that hold deep meaning for us. These symbols can be expressed through tattoos, jewelry, or other forms of personal adornment. Understanding someone's personal symbols can provide insight into their beliefs, experiences, and identity.

Finally, nature itself is full of symbols, from the changing seasons to animals and plants. Understanding these symbols can deepen our connection to the natural world and enhance ecological awareness.

Incorporating Taoist Symbolism in Daily Life

Incorporating Taoist symbolism into daily life is a meaningful practice that aligns with the principles of Taoism. Taoist symbols carry deep meanings, often representing aspects of the natural world, the interconnectedness of opposites, and the pursuit of balance.

Here are some ways to integrate Taoist symbolism into your daily routine:

- **Yin and Yang Awareness:** Embrace the concept of Yin and Yang, symbolized by the interplay of opposites. Recognize the balance between light and darkness, activity and rest, and other dualities in your daily life. Cultivate an awareness of how these forces manifest in your thoughts, actions, and surroundings.

- **Mandala Meditation:** Use mandalas, circular symbols often associated with Taoist philosophy, as a focal point for meditation. Mandalas can represent the cyclical nature of existence and the interconnectedness of all things. Create or find mandalas that resonate with you and incorporate them into your meditation practice.

- **Five Elements Representation:** Understand the symbolism of the five elements in Taoism: Wood, Fire, Earth, Metal, and Water. Recognize these elements in your environment and daily activities. For instance, incorporate wooden or metal objects into your decor, pay attention to the quality of water you consume, or spend time in nature to connect with the Earth element.

- **Natural Imagery in Decor:** Decorate your living space with elements inspired by nature. Taoist symbolism often draws from the natural world, so consider incorporating images of mountains, rivers, trees, and other natural elements into your home or workspace. This can create a serene and harmonious atmosphere.

- **Tao Te Ching Reflection:** Read and reflect on passages from the Tao Te Ching, the foundational text of Taoism attributed to Laozi. Extract symbols and concepts from the text and contemplate how they apply to your daily life. Consider keeping a journal to record your thoughts and insights.

- **Taoist-inspired Art and Crafts:** Engage in artistic expressions inspired by Taoist symbolism. Create paintings, drawings, or crafts that incorporate symbols such as the Tai Chi symbol, the Bagua, or representations of natural elements. Expressing these symbols through art can deepen your connection to Taoist principles.

- **Nature Walks with Mindfulness:** Take nature walks with a mindful approach. Observe the natural world around you, paying attention to the balance and flow of energy. Taoist philosophy encourages a deep connection with nature, and a mindful walk can serve as a daily practice of aligning with the Tao.

- **Tai Chi or Qigong Practice:** Incorporate Tai Chi or Qigong into your daily routine. These traditional Chinese martial arts are deeply rooted in Taoist principles, emphasizing the cultivation of life energy (Qi) and harmonizing movement with breath. Regular practice can help you embody Taoist symbolism in your physical activities.

- **Tea Ceremony:** Embrace the Taoist philosophy of simplicity and mindfulness through a tea ceremony. Use it as an opportunity to savor the present moment, appreciate the natural elements in tea, and cultivate a sense of inner peace and balance.

- **Mindful Eating:** Approach your meals with mindfulness, acknowledging the nourishment provided by the Earth. Consider the qualities of the food you consume, its origins, and the energy it provides. Eating in harmony with Taoist principles involves gratitude and awareness.

Incorporating Taoist symbolism into daily life is a personal and contemplative practice. By infusing your routine with these symbolic elements, you can deepen your connection to the principles of Taoism and cultivate a more harmonious and balanced way of living.

CHAPTER 10

Taoism and Health

Taoism seeks to promote overall well-being by cultivating a balanced and holistic approach to life, including physical health.

Here are several key aspects of integrating Taoist principles for physical well-being:

- **Harmony with Nature:** Taoism encourages us to align ourselves with the natural rhythms of the universe. This involves recognizing and respecting the cyclical nature of life, the changing seasons, and the interconnectedness of all things. Practicing physical activities outdoors, such as walking or tai chi in natural settings, can help attune ourselves to the harmony of nature.

- **Balancing Yin and Yang:** Taoism recognizes the concept of Yin and Yang, representing the dualistic nature of existence. Yin is associated with receptivity, rest, and calmness, while Yang is associated with activity, movement, and energy. Balancing these opposing forces is crucial for physical well-being. Incorporating a mix of activities that include both relaxation and moderate exercise, such as qigong or yoga, helps maintain this equilibrium.

- **Qi Cultivation:** Taoist philosophy places great importance on the cultivation and circulation of qi, the vital life energy. Practices such as qigong and tai chi are designed to enhance the flow of qi throughout the body, promoting physical health and vitality. These gentle, flowing movements aim to balance and harmonize the body's energy, contributing to overall well-being.

- **Mind-Body Connection:** Taoist principles emphasize the interconnectedness of the mind and body. Mental and emotional well-being are considered integral to physical health. Practices like meditation and mindfulness are central to Taoist philosophy, helping individuals achieve a calm and focused mind, which, in turn, positively impacts physical health.

- **Moderation and Simplicity:** Taoism encourages a lifestyle of moderation and simplicity. This applies to both diet and exercise. Eating a balanced, whole foods-based diet in moderation aligns with Taoist principles. Similarly, engaging in moderate physical activities rather than extreme or excessive exercise helps maintain balance and prevents the depletion of vital energy.

- **Embracing Change:** The Taoist concept of "wu wei" advocates for effortless action and going with the natural flow of life. Embracing change and adapting to the inevitable ups and downs of life is essential for physical well-being. Resisting or fighting against the natural order can lead to stress and imbalance. Cultivating flexibility, both physically and mentally, promotes a healthier and more resilient body.

- **Awareness of Body Signals:** Taoist practices emphasize the importance of tuning into the body's signals and listening to its needs. Paying attention to how our bodies responds to various activities, foods, and environments allows us to make choices that support our well-being. This self-awareness is crucial for maintaining a healthy and balanced physical state.

Integrating Taoist principles for physical well-being involves adopting a holistic and mindful approach to life. By harmonizing with nature, balancing opposing forces, cultivating qi, and embracing simplicity and change, we can achieve a state of overall health and vitality.

Dietary Practices and Mindful Eating

Embarking on the journey of dietary practices and mindful eating is about understanding nutrition, cultural influences, and the profound art of savoring each bite. In this section, let's delve into the intricacies of how what we eat and how we eat contribute to our overall well-being.

Remember, dietary choices are not just about satisfying hunger; they play a crucial role in sustaining bodily functions, providing energy, and influencing our long-term health.

Mindful Eating Unveiled

Enter the realm of mindful eating—a practice that extends beyond the mechanical act of consuming food. It's a mindful approach to nourishment that invites us to be fully present, engaging our senses in the symphony of flavors, textures, and aromas that each meal offers.

Mindful eating is a transformative experience where every bite becomes a conscious act, fostering a deeper connection between the mind and the food on our plates. It's a departure from mindless consumption to a mindful embrace of the present moment during meals.

However, it's important to remember that the foods we choose not only impact physical health but also influence mental well-being. The realization that nutritional choices can affect mood, cognitive function, and energy levels highlights the holistic nature of our dietary practices.

By acknowledging this connection, we open the door to reflective eating—an awareness of how food influences not just our bodies but our overall state of mind.

In the vast landscape of dietary information, it's essential to navigate through common myths and misconceptions. Separating evidence-based knowledge from fad diets and sensationalized advice is key to making informed dietary choices.

Of course, our culinary heritage influences not only what we eat but how we approach food. Recognizing and celebrating cultural diversity in dietary practices enriches our understanding of nutrition.

Mindful Eating Techniques

Imagine the practice of slow and deliberate eating—a technique embedded in mindful eating. By embracing a slower pace during meals, we enhance the sensory experience of eating, allowing for better digestion and an increased awareness of satiety.

Portion awareness becomes another technique, encouraging us to understand and respect the body's signals of hunger and fullness. Mindful eating shifts our focus from mindless consumption to a conscious and balanced approach to portion control.

In mindful eating, habits are cultivated with intention. Conscious food choices extend beyond the mere act of selecting what goes on our plates. They encompass considerations of nutritional content, sourcing, and environmental impact.

Gratitude becomes a guiding principle, encouraging us to appreciate the effort and resources involved in bringing each meal to our tables. This mindful approach fosters a deeper connection not only to the food but also to the broader food system.

Addressing Emotional Eating

Emotional eating, often intertwined with our relationship with food, can be addressed through heightened emotional awareness. Recognizing emotional triggers for eating provides an opportunity to develop healthier coping mechanisms.

Embracing non-judgment is a crucial aspect of mindful eating, encouraging us to release guilt associated with certain foods. It invites a balanced perspective, allowing us to enjoy a variety of foods in moderation without falling into the trap of restrictive thinking.

Taoist Approaches to Holistic Health

Taoism views health not merely as the absence of illness but as a harmonious balance of mind, body, and spirit.

At the heart of Taoist philosophy is the concept of the Tao, the ever-flowing and unchanging source of all that exists. Holistic health, in the Taoist perspective, is about aligning with this cosmic force. It transcends the physical and extends to the emotional, mental, and spiritual dimensions of our existence.

Understanding health as a dynamic interplay of energies, Taoism advocates for a balanced and harmonious life that resonates with the natural order of the universe.

Within this, the dynamic interplay of Yin and Yang energies forms the bedrock of understanding balance. Holistic health, according to Taoist principles, is achieved by harmonizing these opposing yet complementary forces. Yin, representing receptivity and stillness, must find equilibrium with Yang, symbolizing activity and dynamism. Taoists seek to balance these energies not just within the body but in all aspects of life as well, fostering a state of equilibrium that resonates with the Tao.

Cultivating the Three Treasures: Jing, Qi, and Shen

Taoist approaches to health extend beyond the physical realm, acknowledging the interconnectedness of mind, body, and spirit. The cultivation of the Three Treasures—Jing (essence), Qi (energy), and Shen (spirit)—is central to this holistic perspective.

Cultivating these treasures involves practices like Qigong, Tai Chi, and meditation, aligning with the Taoist belief that true health arises from a harmonious integration of physical vitality, mental clarity, and spiritual awareness.

Also central to Taoist approaches to health is the principle of Wu Wei. It encourages individuals to flow with the natural rhythms of life, avoiding unnecessary resistance and stress. In the context of health, Wu Wei suggests that forcing wellness may be counterproductive. Instead, Taoists advocate for embracing a state of ease, allowing the body and mind to find their natural balance.

Mind-Body Connection through Meditation

Meditation is a cornerstone of Taoist practices for holistic health. Techniques like Zhan Zhuang (standing meditation) and Daoist meditation aim to foster a deep connection between the mind and the body. Through mindful stillness, Taoists believe one can harmonize internal energies and cultivate a peaceful state of being.

Meditation serves as a tool to quiet the mind, release tension, and attune ourselves to the subtle energies of the Tao, promoting holistic well-being.

Nutritional Wisdom

Taoist dietary practices are rooted in the belief that food is not just sustenance for the body but also a source of energy that can either harmonize or disrupt the flow of Qi. Mindful and balanced nutrition is considered crucial for maintaining health in alignment with the Tao.

Taoist dietary wisdom encourages moderation, simplicity, and an awareness of the energetic qualities of different foods to support overall well-being.

Cultivating Virtue and Compassion

Holistic health in Taoism is not only about the individual but extends to the relational and ethical dimensions of life. Cultivating virtues like compassion, kindness, and humility is seen as essential for overall well-being.

By fostering positive relationships and contributing to the well-being of others, we align ourselves with the Tao and, in turn, promote our own holistic health.

It is a philosophy that embraces the interconnectedness of mind, body, and spirit, inviting us to align with the natural order of the universe. Through the harmonization of energies, mindful practices, and virtuous living, Taoism presents a holistic path to health that resonates with the eternal flow of the Tao.

CHAPTER 11

Taoism and the Art of Tea

In the serene world of Taoism and tea culture, a connection unfolds—a link between ancient philosophy and the art of brewing, sipping, and appreciating tea. This exploration takes us on a journey where the rituals of tea align harmoniously with the principles of the Tao, creating a space where tranquility, mindfulness, and the appreciation of the present moment converge.

We know that at the heart of Taoism lies the concept of the Tao, an ever-flowing, unnamable force that underlies and unites all things. This philosophy values simplicity, balance, and harmony with the natural order. Similarly, the art of tea in Chinese culture encapsulates these very principles.

Tea, in Taoist understanding, is more than a beverage; it is a conduit for connecting with the essence of nature, embodying simplicity, and fostering a sense of balance and harmony in the act of preparation and consumption.

Wu Wei in Tea Preparation

The principle of Wu Wei, or effortless action, finds expression in the meticulous yet seemingly effortless preparation of tea. In Taoism, Wu Wei encourages a state of "non-doing," allowing actions to unfold naturally. Similarly, the tea ceremony embodies this principle as tea masters gracefully perform each step with a calm and unhurried demeanor.

Tea preparation becomes a meditative practice, where every movement, from heating the water to pouring and steeping the leaves, aligns with the Taoist ideal of letting things happen in their own time.

Yin and Yang in Tea Varieties

The Yin and Yang duality, representing balance and opposites, finds reflection in the diverse world of tea. From delicate white teas to robust black teas, the spectrum of flavors and characteristics embodies the harmonious interplay of Yin and Yang energies.

Taoists appreciate this diversity, understanding that each tea variety offers a unique experience, yet collectively they form a balanced tapestry, much like the interdependence of Yin and Yang.

Mindfulness in Tea Consumption

Taoist teachings emphasize the importance of being present in the moment—a concept seamlessly integrated into tea culture. The act of sipping tea becomes a mindful meditation, an opportunity to be fully aware of the aroma, taste, and sensations that unfold with each sip.

By fostering mindfulness in tea consumption, we align ourselves with the Tao, cultivating a deeper appreciation for the beauty inherent in simplicity.

Cultivating Tranquility in Tea Spaces

Taoist principles extend to the spaces where tea is enjoyed. Tea rooms are designed to evoke tranquility, simplicity, and a connection to nature. Elements like natural materials, soothing colors, and minimalist aesthetics, create an environment that harmonizes with the Tao.

These tea spaces become sanctuaries for contemplation, reflection, and communion with the timeless wisdom embedded in both Taoism and tea culture.

Of course, Taoism celebrates the wisdom found in nature, and this is vividly expressed in traditional tea gardens. These carefully designed spaces capture the essence of the natural world, integrating elements like rocks, water features, and plants to evoke a sense of balance and harmony.

Tea gardens become extensions of Taoist philosophy, inviting individuals to connect with nature while indulging in the timeless ritual of tea.

The Tao of Tea Utensils:

In the world of tea, each utensil carries significance beyond its functional purpose. From the teapot to the teacup, every element is chosen with intention, echoing the Taoist belief that every object can embody the principles of balance and simplicity.

Taoists recognize the beauty in the uncarved block—the natural state of things before excessive intervention. Similarly, tea utensils embrace simplicity and natural aesthetics.

Rituals of Tea Preparation and Consumption

Let's take a deeper look at the nuances of Taoist tea ceremonies, revealing how each element contributes to a harmonious and intentional practice.

At the heart of Taoism lies a reverence for simplicity—the beauty found in the unadorned and essential. This principle permeates every aspect of Taoist tea rituals. From the selection of utensils to the deliberate movements in tea preparation, followers aim to capture the essence of simplicity, aligning with the Taoist pursuit of natural harmony.

Taoists see balance as a fundamental aspect of existence, and this equilibrium is reflected in the choice and use of tea utensils. Each utensil, from the teapot to the teacup, is selected with intention, embodying the harmony of Yin and Yang. The careful arrangement of these tools becomes a symbolic expression of the Taoist belief in the interconnectedness of opposites.

Ultimately, tea consumption transcends a simple act of drinking; it becomes a form of meditation—an invitation to savor the present moment. Mindful sipping encourages us to fully engage our senses, appreciating the flavors, aromas, and textures present in each cup. Within this, the act of tea consumption aligns with the Taoist philosophy of being fully present and attuned to the simplicity of the immediate experience.

Finding Mindfulness and Tranquility in Tea Ceremonies

Let's now understand how each carefully orchestrated movement and sip invites us into a state of profound presence and inner calm.

Tea ceremonies often commence with a deliberate and mindful preparation of the tea leaves—a prelude to the contemplative journey ahead. Every step, from measuring the leaves to heating the water, is a conscious act that signals the beginning of a meditative practice. In this ritual of preparation, we are encouraged to be fully present, setting the stage for the tranquility that unfolds.

As the tea is poured into the vessel, the principle of Wu Wei, or effortless action, becomes palpable. Tea masters execute each pour with grace, mirroring the natural flow of water. This act of pouring becomes a metaphor for letting go of resistance and allowing things to unfold organically—a lesson in the art of effortless living. Participants are invited to synchronize their minds with the gentle rhythm of the pour, cultivating a sense of inner calm.

The selection and use of tea utensils contribute significantly to the mindful atmosphere of the ceremony. Each utensil, whether it's the delicate teapot or the intricately crafted teacup, is chosen with intention. Participants are encouraged to observe and appreciate the aesthetic beauty of these tools, fostering a sense of gratitude for the simplicity and elegance they bring to the ceremony. Utensils become instruments of contemplation, grounding us in the present moment.

Mindful Consumption: Savoring Each Sip

The heart of mindfulness in tea ceremonies lies in the act of consumption. As participants lift the teacup to their lips, they are urged to engage their senses fully. The warmth of the cup, the aroma of the steeped leaves, and the nuanced flavors of the tea become focal points of awareness. Mindful sipping encourages a deliberate and unhurried pace, allowing us to savor each moment and taste. In this way, tea consumption becomes a form of meditation—a practice in being fully present.

Silence and Contemplation: The Space Between Sips

A notable feature of tea ceremonies is the emphasis on silence and contemplation. The pauses between sips are not filled with idle chatter but rather with stillness. Participants are encouraged to turn their attention inward, reflecting on the sensations and thoughts that arise with each sip. This intentional silence creates a sacred space for introspection and invites a profound connection with our inner self.

Tea Spaces: Environments of Tranquility

The physical setting of a tea ceremony plays a crucial role in creating an environment conducive to mindfulness. Tea spaces are often designed with natural elements, soothing colors, and minimalist aesthetics, evoking a sense of tranquility. The intentional arrangement of these spaces serves as a gentle reminder to be present, fostering an atmosphere where we can disconnect from the outside world and immerse ourselves in the serenity of the moment.

Cultivating Inner Calm: The Culmination of Mindful Tea Practice

The culmination of a mindful tea ceremony is the cultivation of inner calm. Participants, having engaged in every aspect of the ceremony with mindful awareness, often emerge with a heightened sense of tranquility. The rhythmic and intentional nature of the tea ritual serves as a meditative journey—a brief respite from the hustle and bustle of everyday life. This practice becomes a sanctuary for us to reconnect with our inner selves and find solace in the simplicity of the present moment.

Carrying Mindfulness Beyond the Ceremony: An Invitation to Daily Practice

The lessons of mindfulness and tranquility gleaned from tea ceremonies are not confined to the duration of the ritual. We are encouraged to carry the essence of mindfulness into our daily lives. The intentional and present-moment awareness cultivated during tea ceremonies becomes a guiding principle—a source of balance and calm amid life's challenges.

From the initial ritual of preparation to the contemplative moments between sips, each element is carefully designed to draw us into a state of presence and inner calm. The tea ceremony becomes a haven—a sacred space where we can momentarily step away from the noise of the world and discover the serenity that resides within. In the simplicity of a cup of tea, a profound practice unfolds—a practice that invites us to savor the beauty of each moment, one mindful sip at a time.

CHAPTER 12

Taoism in Art and Literature

In Chinese cultural heritage, Taoism emerges as a guiding force, shaping the contours and strokes of traditional Chinese arts with its deep philosophies. In this chapter, we will delve into the nuanced ways in which Taoism has left its imprint on various artistic expressions, from painting and calligraphy to poetry and performing arts.

Taoist Philosophy and Artistic Expression

The concept of the Tao profoundly influences traditional Chinese arts. Artists, inspired by Taoist philosophies, seek to capture the essence of the Tao in their creations, emphasizing harmony, balance, and the natural order.

The Taoist principle of Wu Wei, or effortless action, finds vivid expression in Chinese calligraphy and painting. Artists cultivate a state of non-interference, allowing their brushstrokes to flow naturally and spontaneously. The blank canvas becomes a realm where the artist engages in a dance of ink and paper, embodying the Taoist ideal of letting things happen in their own time and with graceful ease.

Yin and Yang in Balance

The duality of Yin and Yang, representing opposites and balance, manifests prominently in traditional Chinese arts. Whether in landscape paintings or porcelain designs, artists skillfully juxtapose elements to create a harmonious equilibrium. The interplay of light and dark, solid and void, reflects the Taoist understanding of the complementary forces inherent in the natural world.

Taoist reverence for nature finds profound expression in the landscape painting tradition. Artists aim not merely to replicate scenery but to convey the spirit and energy of the natural world. The mist-covered mountains, meandering rivers, and solitary trees become metaphors for the eternal cycle of life and the interconnectedness celebrated by Taoism.

Empty Spaces and Meaningful Silence

Taoist influence is discernible in the strategic use of empty spaces within artworks, be it a painting or a poem. These blank spaces are not voids but deliberate pauses, inviting the viewer or reader to engage in contemplation.

In the silence between brushstrokes or lines of verse, Taoism speaks, emphasizing the beauty found in simplicity and the unspoken depth within the void.

Dance and Theatre as Dynamic Taoist Expressions

Traditional Chinese performing arts, including dance and theater, also bear the mark of Taoist influence. The fluid movements in traditional dance, reminiscent of nature's rhythms, align with the Taoist principle of flow.

In traditional theater, themes often revolve around the search for balance and the harmonious resolution of conflicts—a narrative reflection of Taoist ideals.

The Tao of Tea in Ceramics

Ceramics, a celebrated form of Chinese art, embodies the Taoist appreciation for the uncarved block. In the creation of teaware, potters embrace simplicity and natural aesthetics. Each teapot or tea cup becomes a vessel not just for tea but for the embodiment of

Taoist principles—balance, harmony, and the beauty found in the unadorned.

Poetry as a Path to the Tao

Taoist themes echo through classical Chinese poetry, where poets seek to convey the ineffable and capture the transient beauty of existence. The brevity and simplicity of classical poetry align with Taoist notions of the unspoken depth within simplicity. Through carefully chosen words, poets invite readers to contemplate the mysteries of the Tao.

Theatricality and Ritual in Martial Arts

Martial arts, deeply intertwined with Chinese culture, draw inspiration from Taoist philosophies. The fluid movements, emphasis on internal energy (Qi), and the pursuit of martial harmony reflect the Taoist belief in the interconnectedness of mind, body, and nature. Martial arts become a dynamic expression of Wu Wei, where followers learn to act without unnecessary effort.

Culinary Arts: The Tao of Chinese Cuisine

Even in the culinary realm, the influence of Taoism is evident. Traditional Chinese cuisine, with its emphasis on balance in flavors, textures, and colors, mirrors the Taoist principle of Yin and Yang. The art of Chinese cooking seeks to harmonize contrasting elements to create a balanced and nourishing culinary experience.

Overall, the influence of Taoism on traditional Chinese arts is profound and enduring. Beyond being aesthetic expressions, these art forms become conduits for conveying the timeless wisdom of the Tao. Whether through the fluid brushstrokes of a landscape painting, the meditative choreography of a traditional dance, or the carefully crafted verses of a poem, Taoism continues to shape and enrich the cultural tapestry of China, inviting us to contemplate the interconnected beauty of existence.

Literary Works Inspired by Taoist Philosophy

The essence of Taoist philosophy, with its emphasis on simplicity, harmony, and the interconnectedness of all things, has been a wellspring of inspiration for countless literary minds throughout history. Let's take a look at the profound impact of Taoism on literary works, examining how this ancient philosophy has woven its subtle threads into the fabric of poetry, prose, and philosophical writings.

As previously mentioned, at the forefront of Taoist literary contributions stands the seminal work, the Tao Te Ching, attributed to Laozi. Comprising 81 succinct chapters, this foundational text encapsulates the core tenets of Taoism. Its verses, shrouded in poetic ambiguity, explore the nature of the Tao, the virtue of simplicity, and the power of non-action (Wu Wei). The Tao Te Ching serves not only as a philosophical guide but as a poetic masterpiece that has resonated through the ages.

Zhuangzi's Playful Parables

Zhuangzi, another luminary in the Taoist tradition, contributed a collection of whimsical and thought-provoking parables in his eponymous work. With allegorical tales and philosophical dialogues, Zhuangzi explores the relativity of perception, the illusory nature of distinctions, and the joy of embracing the Daoist concept of "going with the flow." His writings are a literary puzzle where wisdom is interwoven with humor and paradox.

Nature's Tapestry: Poetry and Taoism

Taoist philosophy, deeply rooted in a reverence for nature, has found exquisite expression in Chinese poetry. Poets like Wang Wei, Li Bai, and Du Fu infused their verses with the spirit of Taoism. Nature in their poetry is not just scenery but a living manifestation of the Tao. The rustling of leaves, the flow of rivers, and the solitude of mountains become metaphors for the timeless principles of Yin and Yang, impermanence, and the cyclical nature of existence.

The Dream of the Red Chamber: Taoist Themes in Fiction

Even in the realm of fiction, Taoist themes have left an indelible mark. "The Dream of the Red Chamber" by Cao Xueqin, considered one of China's greatest novels, subtly includes Taoist principles into its narrative. The novel explores the transience of life, the illusory nature of wealth and power, and the interconnectedness of characters in a complex, ever-changing world.

The Tao in Modern Literature

The influence of Taoism extends beyond classical works into modern literature. Authors such as Ursula K. Le Guin, with her novel, "The Dispossessed," draw upon Taoist ideas to explore themes of balance, harmony, and the search for utopia. The concept of balance, central to Taoism, finds resonance in characters navigating the delicate equilibrium of their worlds.

Alan Watts: Bridging East and West

In the 20th century, philosopher and writer Alan Watts played a pivotal role in introducing Eastern philosophies, including Taoism, to a Western audience. Through books like "The Way of Zen," Watts conveyed Taoist concepts in a manner accessible to Western readers, facilitating a cross-cultural exchange of ideas and influencing a generation of thinkers.

The Tao in Beat Poetry: Gary Snyder

In the Beat Generation, poet Gary Snyder drew inspiration from Taoist principles. His poems, often immersed in the contemplation of nature and the interdependence of all things, reflect the Taoist ethos. Snyder's deep engagement with Zen Buddhism, itself influenced by Taoism, adds layers of philosophical richness to his poetic works.

Philosophical Dialogues: Modern Taoist Literature

Contemporary authors engage in philosophical dialogues influenced by Taoism. Works like "The Tao of Pooh" by Benjamin Hoff use the beloved character Winnie the Pooh to convey Taoist wisdom in an accessible and charming manner. These dialogues bridge the ancient philosophy with modern thought, making the profound concepts of Taoism approachable to a wider audience.

As you can see, Taoist philosophy, with its timeless principles and poetic nuances, has left an enduring legacy in literature. From the ancient wisdom of Laozi and Zhuangzi to the evocative verses of Chinese poets, and from classical novels to modern philosophical dialogues, the influence of Taoism resonates through the ink of literary works.

These writings not only encapsulate the essence of Taoist thought but also invite us to contemplate the subtle rhythms of the Tao, encouraging a deeper understanding of the interconnected nature of existence.

Exploring Visual Representations of Taoist Concepts

Delving into visual arts, the exploration of Taoist concepts becomes an exquisite combination of symbols and compositions that seek to capture the ineffable essence of the Tao. This extensive examination traverses the rich landscapes of traditional Chinese painting, calligraphy, and contemporary visual representations to uncover how artists, across centuries, have grappled with expressing the intangible principles of Taoism.

Chinese Landscape Painting: Nature as a Manifestation of the Tao

Traditional Chinese landscape painting stands as a testament to the profound influence of Taoist philosophy. Artists, inspired by the Tao, embark on a visual journey that transcends mere representation.

The mist-shrouded mountains, meandering rivers, and solitary trees are not just scenery but symbols of the eternal dance of Yin and Yang, the cyclical nature of existence, and the interconnectedness of all things. The empty spaces within the paintings invite viewers to contemplate the uncarved block—the essence of the Tao.

Wu Wei in Brushstrokes: The Art of Effortless Action

The principle of Wu Wei, or effortless action, finds its expression in the fluid and spontaneous brushstrokes of Chinese calligraphy. Calligraphers, often embodying the role of the Taoist sage, allow their brushes to dance across the paper with grace and fluidity. The characters become more than words—they are visual poetry, capturing the essence of the Tao through the intentional emptiness and the effortless flow of ink.

Yin and Yang on Silk: Balancing Opposites in Silk Painting

Silk painting, with its vibrant hues and delicate textures, becomes a canvas for exploring the interplay of Yin and Yang. Artists harmonize opposites—light and dark, bold and subtle—in their compositions. The silk itself, a luxurious and smooth surface, echoes the Taoist appreciation for the uncarved block, inviting viewers to touch upon the silk threads of the Tao.

Daoist Symbolism in Traditional Art: The Eight Immortals and Beyond

Traditional Chinese art often incorporates Daoist symbolism, and the depictions of the Eight Immortals stand as iconic representations. Each immortal embodies a facet of Daoist philosophy—Longevity, Harmony, and Enlightenment. The visual narratives of these immortals convey not only their mythical tales but also serve as allegories for the pursuit of Daoist virtues and the journey towards the Tao.

Contemporary Visualizations: From Watercolor to Digital Art

In the contemporary art scene, artists continue to explore Taoist concepts through a myriad of mediums. Watercolor artists evoke the flowing nature of water, reflecting the Taoist principle of adaptability. Digital artists create immersive, interactive installations that invite participants to experience the principles of Wu Wei and interconnectedness in a dynamic, modern context.

Taoist Temples as Living Art: Architectural Embodiments of the Tao

Taoist temples, with their intricate designs and harmonious layouts, are themselves visual representations of Taoist concepts. The architectural symbolism, from the circular roofs representing the heavens to the interconnected courtyards embodying the unity of Yin and Yang, speaks volumes about the Taoist worldview. The temple becomes a living canvas where devotees can visually engage with the principles they seek to embody.

Contemplative Photography: Capturing the Tao in Stillness

Photographers, influenced by Taoist thought, employ their lenses to capture moments of stillness and contemplation. The play of light and shadow, the harmony found in the convergence of elements, and the focus on the present moment all echo the Taoist emphasis on mindfulness and the appreciation of the ordinary. Photographs become visual haikus, encapsulating the essence of the Tao in a single frame.

Martial Arts Choreography: The Movement of Tao in Motion

Martial arts, deeply intertwined with Taoist philosophy, translate the principles of the Tao into physical movements. The choreography of martial arts becomes a visual representation of Wu Wei—an embodiment of effortless action and harmony. The fluidity of Tai

Chi or the precision of Kung Fu reflects the Taoist belief in the interconnectedness of mind, body, and nature.

Visual representations of Taoist concepts span centuries and mediums, encapsulating the fluidity and depth of this ancient philosophy. These artistic manifestations not only serve as windows into the profound world of Taoist thought but also invite viewers to embark on their own visual journeys, contemplating the timeless principles encapsulated in the interplay of form and emptiness, color and void—a harmonious dance that echoes the Tao itself.

CHAPTER 13

Taoism and Contemporary Living

As we navigate the complexities of the modern world, the ancient wisdom of Taoism offers a beacon of guidance. Let's try and understand the ways we can adapt Taoist principles to cultivate balance, mindfulness, and harmony in our contemporary lives, and make everyday challenges a little easier to handle.

Wu Wei in Action: Effortless Living in a Busy World

In the hustle and bustle of modern life, the principle of Wu Wei, or effortless action, becomes a guiding light. Rather than succumbing to the pressures of constant productivity, we can embrace a more balanced approach. Wu Wei encourages recognizing and flowing with the natural rhythms of life, allowing decisions and actions to unfold with grace and ease. By relinquishing the need for forceful control, we can navigate challenges with a sense of calm and adaptability.

Yin and Yang in Work-Life Balance

Taoist philosophy places a profound emphasis on the harmony between opposites—Yin and Yang. In the context of modern life, striking a balance between work and personal life becomes paramount. The ceaseless demands of work can be counteracted by moments of rest and rejuvenation. Recognizing the interdependence of these opposites fosters a holistic approach to well-being, preventing burnout and promoting sustainable success.

Embracing Simplicity in a Complex World

In a world inundated with stimuli and constant connectivity, the Taoist virtue of simplicity becomes a powerful antidote. Adapting this principle involves decluttering not just physical spaces but also mental and emotional landscapes. Simplifying daily routines, focusing on essential tasks, and embracing the beauty of the unadorned contribute to a sense of clarity and tranquility amid the noise of modernity.

Cultivating Mindfulness in the Digital Age

The rapid pace of technological advancements and information overload can lead to a fragmented sense of attention. Taoist principles advocate for mindfulness—a deliberate presence in each moment. Techniques such as meditation, conscious breathing, and mindful awareness enable us to center ourselves amidst the digital distractions.

By fostering a mindful approach, we can enhance focus, reduce stress, and deepen our connection with the present.

Adaptability and the Art of Water

Water, often used as a metaphor in Taoist teachings, symbolizes adaptability and resilience. In modern life, adapting Taoist principles involves cultivating a similar fluidity in facing challenges. Instead of resisting change, we can embrace an adaptable mindset, navigating the currents of life with flexibility. Like water that shapes itself to the container it occupies, adapting to circumstances with a fluid approach fosters a sense of empowerment.

Interconnected Living: Nurturing Relationships

Taoist principles emphasize the interconnectedness of all things. In the context of modern relationships, this involves fostering genuine connections and cultivating empathy. By recognizing the interconnected nature of humanity, we can approach relationships with compassion, understanding, and a sense of shared humanity. The cultivation of harmonious connections contributes to a more balanced and fulfilling life.

Eco-conscious Living: Aligning with Nature

Taoism's deep connection with nature encourages us to align our lifestyles with ecological principles. Adapting Taoist teachings involves adopting sustainable practices, reducing environmental impact, and appreciating the interconnected relationship between humans and the natural world. By living in harmony with nature, we contribute to a more sustainable and balanced global ecosystem.

Personal Development through Inner Cultivation

Taoist philosophy places a significant emphasis on inner cultivation for personal development. Modern life offers various avenues for self-discovery, from engaging in mindfulness practices to pursuing creative endeavors. The pursuit of self-awareness, personal growth, and a deeper understanding of our own nature aligns with Taoist principles, contributing to a more fulfilling and purposeful life.

Balancing Ambition with Contentment

In a society that often glorifies ambition and achievement, Taoist principles encourage us to balance ambition with contentment. The pursuit of goals can coexist with a profound appreciation for the present moment. By cultivating contentment, we can find joy in the journey, fostering a sense of fulfillment that transcends external achievements.

Holistic Health: Integrating Mind, Body, and Spirit

Taoist principles underscore the interconnectedness of mind, body, and spirit. Adapting these principles involves prioritizing holistic health—nourishing the body with balanced nutrition, engaging in mindful movement practices, and cultivating mental and emotional well-being. The integration of these aspects contributes to a harmonious and balanced approach to personal health.

In summary, adapting Taoist principles to modern life involves a conscious and intentional application of ancient wisdom to the complexities of contemporary existence. By embracing Wu Wei, finding balance in opposites, and aligning with the natural order, we can navigate the challenges of the modern world with a sense of ease, mindfulness, and harmony.

The timeless teachings of Taoism continue to serve as a source of inspiration for those seeking a more balanced and purposeful life in the 21st century.

Balancing Technology and Simplicity

We live in a world that is focused almost entirely on technology and the quest for a balanced lifestyle becomes increasingly difficult yet relevant. Striking a harmonious equilibrium between the benefits of technology and the virtue of simplicity is a modern day challenge that warrants thoughtful consideration.

Let's take a closer look at how we can use Taoist principles to find balance in a world where the digital and the simple intersect.

Embracing the Digital Landscape

Firstly, it's important to note the benefits of technology. The pervasive influence of technology has undeniably transformed the way we live, work, and communicate. Smartphones, computers, and the internet have become integral aspects of modern life, offering unprecedented convenience and connectivity. Embracing the digital landscape involves acknowledging the positive impact technology has on efficiency, communication, and access to information.

Amid the myriad digital possibilities, the principle of simplicity emerges as a guiding beacon. Simplicity encourages a deliberate focus on what is essential, an intentional paring down of complexity, and a mindful approach to daily life. It invites us to declutter not just physical spaces but also the digital realms of emails, notifications, and online engagements.

Yet, as technology integrates seamlessly into daily routines, there arises a need for occasional digital detoxes. Mindful consumption of technology involves periods of intentional disconnection to foster mental clarity and emotional well-being. Setting boundaries on screen time, embracing device-free moments, and cultivating awareness of the digital content consumed contribute to a balanced relationship with technology.

The Art of Single-Tasking

In a world that often glorifies multitasking, the Taoist principle of focusing on one thing at a time gains significance. Balancing technology and simplicity involves practicing the art of single-tasking—concentrating fully on one activity without constant digital interruptions. This intentional focus not only enhances productivity but also fosters a sense of mindfulness and presence.

Creating Digital Sanctuaries

Amid the incessant buzz of notifications and information overload, we can carve out digital sanctuaries. Designating specific times or spaces for focused, uninterrupted work or leisure helps in balancing the inundation of digital stimuli. By consciously creating moments of digital quietude, we can cultivate a sense of tranquility and mental clarity.

Mindful Technology Adoption

Balancing technology and simplicity involves a discerning approach to adopting new digital tools. Mindful technology adoption entails evaluating the necessity and impact of each technological addition. Choosing tools that align with personal values, contribute positively to well-being, and serve a meaningful purpose supports a balanced integration of technology into daily life.

Nature as a Counterbalance

Connecting with nature becomes a potent counterbalance to the digital saturation of modern life. Spending time outdoors, away from ever-present screens, allows us to recalibrate and rejuvenate. Nature serves as a reminder of the simplicity and beauty found in the unspoiled, unfiltered world, offering a respite from the complexities of the digital realm.

Digital Mindfulness Practices

Adapting mindfulness practices to the digital realm fosters a balanced relationship with technology. Incorporating digital mindfulness involves being fully present while engaging with screens—whether it's practicing mindful scrolling, setting purposeful intentions for online activities, or employing digital meditation apps. These practices enhance awareness and intentionality in the digital experience.

Designing Digital Minimalism

In pursuit of balance, we can adopt principles of digital minimalism. This involves intentionally minimizing digital clutter, reducing the number of apps and online subscriptions, and decluttering digital spaces. Digital minimalism supports a streamlined, intentional use of technology that aligns with the principles of simplicity.

Cultivating Technological Wisdom

Ultimately, the pursuit of balance between technology and simplicity is an ongoing journey guided by technological wisdom. Cultivating technological wisdom involves continuously reassessing the impact of technology on well-being, relationships, and overall quality of life. It encourages a thoughtful, informed approach to digital engagement that aligns with individual values and the pursuit of a balanced, fulfilling existence.

Balancing technology and simplicity in the digital age is a nuanced endeavor that requires conscious choices and mindful awareness. By embracing the benefits of technology while honoring the virtues of simplicity, we can navigate the complexities of the modern world with intentionality, fostering a harmonious and balanced lifestyle.

The key lies in finding a personalized equilibrium that aligns with individual values, priorities, and the quest for a meaningful, fulfilling life.

Navigating the Challenges of a Fast-Paced World

In the relentless surge of the modern era, where the pace of life often resembles a swift river, we often find ourselves navigating challenges that demand resilience, adaptability, and a strategic approach. This section delves into the many facets of contending with the fast-paced currents of contemporary existence and offers insights into how we can not only survive but thrive in the face of these challenges.

Of course, one of the defining characteristics of a fast-paced world is the rapidity of change. Technological advancements, social shifts, and economic fluctuations occur at an unprecedented speed. Navigating this dynamic landscape requires us to develop a mindset of continual adaptation, embracing change as an inherent aspect of the journey.

Coping with Information Overload

In an age dominated by digital connectivity, the deluge of information can be overwhelming. Navigating the challenges involves developing discernment in information consumption. Cultivating the ability to filter, prioritize, and focus on essential information allows us to maintain clarity and prevent cognitive overload.

Work-Life Integration

The traditional demarcation between work and personal life has blurred in the fast-paced world. Navigating this integration demands a thoughtful balance. Setting boundaries, prioritizing self-care, and recognizing the importance of downtime become crucial strategies in maintaining equilibrium amidst the demands of a career and personal responsibilities.

Stress Management in the Fast Lane

The accelerated pace of life often contributes to heightened stress levels. Navigating stress involves adopting effective coping mechanisms. Mindfulness practices, regular exercise, and fostering a supportive social network become essential tools for managing stress and preventing burnout in the face of relentless demands.

Prioritizing Well-being

In the rush to keep up with the pace, we may neglect our physical and mental well-being. Navigating the challenges requires a conscious commitment to prioritize health. Regular exercise, nutritious eating habits, and sufficient rest contribute not only to physical vitality but also to mental resilience in the face of constant demands.

Cultivating Adaptability

Flexibility and adaptability emerge as indispensable skills for navigating a fast-paced world. The ability to pivot, adjust strategies, and embrace change with resilience ensures that we remain agile amidst the unpredictable currents of life. Cultivating a growth mindset fosters a proactive approach to challenges, viewing them as opportunities for learning and development.

Time Management Strategies

Efficient time management becomes a compass in the fast-paced journey. Navigating the demands of work, personal commitments, and self-care involves prioritizing tasks, setting realistic goals, and embracing tools and techniques that enhance productivity. Time becomes a valuable resource to be invested wisely.

Building Meaningful Connections

Amidst the speed of life, fostering authentic connections becomes a navigational anchor. Building and maintaining meaningful relationships contribute to a sense of support, belonging, and emotional well-being. Cultivating interpersonal skills and investing time in nurturing connections provide a sense of stability in the midst of rapid change.

Embracing Minimalism

In a world saturated with stimuli, embracing minimalism becomes a strategic response. Navigating the challenges involves simplifying one's environment, decluttering both physical and mental spaces, and focusing on the essentials. Minimalism serves as a counterbalance to the excesses of a fast-paced lifestyle.

Mindful Reflection and Pause

Amidst the rush, carving out moments for mindful reflection becomes a crucial navigational tool. Taking intentional pauses, whether through meditation, contemplation, or simply slowing down, allows us to reassess priorities, regain perspective, and recalibrate our course in alignment with their values.

Navigating the challenges of a fast-paced world is an art that requires a combination of strategic thinking, adaptability, and a commitment to personal well-being. By developing a resilient mindset, adopting effective coping mechanisms, and embracing intentional living, we can not only navigate the rapid currents but also find fulfillment, purpose, and a sense of balance amidst the whirlwind of modern life.

CHAPTER 14

Taoism and Interpersonal Relationships

A pplying Taoist principles to relationships can help to bring us closer to our loved ones and develop a strong and enduring connection. We can integrate the ancient Chinese philosophy of Taoism into the dynamics of interpersonal connections.

Here are several key aspects of Taoist principles as they relate to relationships:

- **Harmony with Nature:** Taoism encourages us to align ourselves with the natural flow of life. In relationships, this means embracing the organic development of connections without forcing or resisting. Just as nature unfolds in its own time, relationships are allowed to evolve naturally, fostering a sense of ease and balance.

- **Wu Wei (Non-Action):** The concept of Wu Wei suggests that one should act effortlessly and without unnecessary interference. In relationships, this involves letting go of the need to control or manipulate situations. Instead of forcing outcomes, we are encouraged to trust the natural course of events and allow relationships to unfold spontaneously.

- **Yin and Yang:** Taoism emphasizes the interplay of opposites, represented by the concept of Yin and Yang. In relationships, recognizing and appreciating the complementary nature of opposites is crucial. Rather than viewing differences as obstacles, Taoist principles encourage seeing them as essential elements that contribute to the balance and richness of the relationship.

- **Acceptance and Detachment:** Taoism promotes acceptance of the present moment and detachment from desires and expectations. In relationships, this means letting go of preconceived notions and allowing things to be as they are. Detachment from specific outcomes fosters a sense of contentment and reduces unnecessary conflict.

- **Simplicity:** Taoism advocates for simplicity in life, and this simplicity can be applied to relationships as well. Striving for uncomplicated interactions, clear communication, and minimal external influences can help create an environment where relationships can flourish naturally.

- **Compassion and Kindness:** The Taoist principle of compassion encourages us to approach others with understanding and empathy. In relationships, this translates to kindness, patience, and a willingness to listen. By cultivating a compassionate attitude, conflicts can be resolved more harmoniously, and connections deepened.

- **Inner Balance:** Taoism emphasizes the importance of inner balance, and this is crucial in relationships as well. We are encouraged to cultivate self-awareness, maintain their inner equilibrium, and avoid becoming overly attached or dependent on external factors for happiness.

- **Embracing Change:** The Taoist concept of the ever-changing nature of the Tao encourages us to embrace change rather than resist it. In relationships, adaptability and flexibility are essential for growth. Embracing the natural ebb and flow of connections allows for continued development and evolution.

By integrating these Taoist principles into relationships, we create a more mindful and balanced way of relating to others, ultimately contributing to the well-being of both parties.

Harmony in Family and Community

In Taoism, the concept of harmony in family and community is deeply rooted in the philosophy's emphasis on balance, interconnectedness, and living in accordance with the Tao–the natural order of the universe.

The principles of Taoism provide a framework for us to cultivate harmonious relationships within our families and communities. Here are some key aspects:

- **Respect for Nature's Rhythms:** Taoism encourages us to align ourselves with the natural flow of life. In the context of family and community, this involves recognizing the cyclical nature of relationships, the changing seasons of life, and the importance of adapting to these natural rhythms. By doing so, we can foster a sense of harmony within our familial and communal bonds.

- **Balancing Yin and Yang:** The Taoist concept of Yin and Yang represents the interplay of opposites and the necessity of balance. Within families and communities, recognizing and respecting the complementary aspects of different roles, personalities, and contributions is essential. Each member plays a unique part in maintaining the overall equilibrium.

- **Wu Wei in Relationships:** The principle of Wu Wei, or non-action, encourages us to act in accordance with the natural order of things. In family and community dynamics, this means allowing relationships to unfold organically, without imposing unnecessary control or interference. Wu Wei fosters a sense of ease and spontaneity in interactions.

- **Mutual Support and Interdependence:** Taoism emphasizes the interconnectedness of all things. Within families and communities, this principle underscores the importance of mutual support and interdependence. We are encouraged to recognize and appreciate each other's strengths and weaknesses, working together for the greater well-being of the whole.

- **Humility and Simplicity:** Taoist teachings advocate for humility and simplicity in our approach to life. Applying these principles in family and community interactions involves avoiding unnecessary complexity, ego-driven conflicts, and power struggles. Instead, we are encouraged to embrace a humble and straightforward attitude in our relationships.

- **Compassion and Forgiveness:** Compassion is a core value in Taoism. Within families and communities, cultivating a compassionate mindset promotes understanding, empathy, and forgiveness. Recognizing the imperfections in oneself and others helps to build bridges and resolve conflicts, contributing to a more harmonious environment.

- **Cultivating Inner Harmony:** Taoism places great importance on individual cultivation and inner balance. In the context of families and communities, we are encouraged to cultivate inner virtues, practice self-reflection, and work on personal growth. By achieving inner harmony, we contribute positively to the collective harmony of the family and community.

- **Adapting to Change:** The Taoist perspective on the inevitability of change is applicable to family and community life. Being open to change, adapting to evolving circumstances, and embracing the natural cycles of growth and transformation contribute to the overall harmony within these social units.

By incorporating these Taoist principles into family and community life, we can contribute to creating environments that are characterized by mutual respect, understanding, and a sense of balance. This approach fosters a harmonious coexistence, promoting the well-being and flourishing of all relationships.

Communication and Conflict Resolution

Communication and conflict resolution in Taoism are guided by principles that emphasize harmony, balance, and a deep understanding of the natural order. To help you overcome issues and conflicts in your life, let's take a look at some key aspects of communication and conflict resolution in Taoism:

- **Non-Contention and Wu Wei (Non-Action):** Taoism encourages us to practice non-contention, avoiding unnecessary conflict and confrontation. The principle of Wu Wei suggests that we should act in accordance with the natural flow of events, allowing resolutions to emerge organically. This involves letting go of the need to control or dominate conversations and conflicts.

- **Listening and Understanding:** Effective communication in Taoism involves active listening and seeking to understand others. By approaching conversations with an open mind and genuine curiosity, we can cultivate a deeper awareness of different perspectives. This understanding is essential for preventing and resolving conflicts.

- **Yin and Yang in Dialogue:** The interplay of Yin and Yang is a fundamental concept in Taoism. In communication, recognizing the balance between speaking and listening, expressing and receiving, is crucial. Both parties contribute to the dynamic flow of dialogue, and understanding the harmonious exchange between these elements is key to resolving conflicts.

- **Harmony in Expression:** Taoist communication promotes expressing ourselves in a way that maintains harmony. This involves choosing words carefully, avoiding unnecessary harshness, and being mindful of the impact language can have on relationships. The goal is to communicate assertively without causing undue discord.

- **Embracing Paradox:** Taoism acknowledges the inherent paradoxes in life. In communication, this means embracing the complexity of human interactions and recognizing that opposing viewpoints can coexist. Rather than seeing conflicts as absolute contradictions, we can explore the middle path and find common ground.

- **Compassionate Communication:** Compassion is a core value in Taoism, and it plays a crucial role in conflict resolution. Approaching conflicts with empathy and understanding helps create an atmosphere conducive to resolution. Compassionate communication involves acknowledging emotions, validating concerns, and working together to find solutions.

- **Detachment from Ego:** Taoist principles advocate for detachment from the ego. In conflicts, we are encouraged to set aside personal pride and the need to be right. Detaching from the ego allows for a more objective perspective, fostering a cooperative approach to conflict resolution.

- **Seeking the Middle Way:** The Taoist concept of the Middle Way encourages us to find a balanced and moderate approach. In conflict resolution, this means avoiding extremes and finding compromises that honor the needs and perspectives of all parties involved. The goal is to reach solutions that maintain overall harmony.

- **Cultivating Patience:** Taoism teaches the value of patience and the understanding that everything has its own time. In conflict resolution, patience allows for a thorough exploration of issues and the gradual unfolding of solutions. Rushing the process can lead to incomplete resolutions and lingering tensions.

- **Natural Resolution:** Taoism emphasizes that conflicts, like all aspects of life, are transient. Trusting the natural course of events and allowing time for resolution to unfold aligns with the Taoist principle of going with the flow. This approach involves a level of faith in the natural order of things and a belief that, given time, conflicts can naturally find resolution.

When we incorporate these Taoist principles into communication and conflict resolution, we can navigate disputes with a focus on harmony, understanding, and mutual growth. The aim is not to eliminate conflict entirely but to transform it into an opportunity for positive change and increased harmony within relationships and communities.

CHAPTER 15

The Journey Continues – Further Exploration of Taoism

I f you're interested in delving deeper into the study of Taoism, there are various resources available that can help you gain a comprehensive understanding of its philosophy, history, and practices.

Here's a list of resources across different formats:

Books:

- "Tao Te Ching" by Lao Tzu: The foundational text of Taoism, this classic work provides profound insights into the principles of the Tao. There are numerous translations available; some popular ones include translations by Stephen Mitchell, D.C. Lau, and Ursula K. Le Guin.

- "Chuang Tzu" by Chuang Tzu: Another essential Taoist text, "Chuang Tzu" explores the ideas of individualism, spontaneity, and the relativity of things. Translations by Burton Watson and Thomas Merton are highly regarded.

- "The Tao of Pooh" by Benjamin Hoff: This book combines Taoist philosophy with the beloved characters from A.A. Milne's Winnie-the-Pooh stories, making it an accessible introduction to Taoist principles.

- "The Taoist Classics: The Collected Translations of Thomas Cleary" by Thomas Cleary: This collection brings together translations of key Taoist texts, providing a comprehensive overview of Taoist thought.

Online Resources:

- Internet Encyclopedia of Philosophy - Taoism: An online resource providing in-depth articles on various aspects of Taoism, its history, philosophy, and key figures. https://www.iep.utm.edu/taoism/

- Stanford Encyclopedia of Philosophy - Daoism: Stanford's philosophy encyclopedia offers scholarly articles on Daoism, covering historical developments and major philosophical ideas. https://plato.stanford.edu/entries/daoism/

Courses and Lectures:

- "Taoism 101: Introduction to the Tao" (Online Course): Offered by various online learning platforms, this course provides a structured introduction to Taoism, covering its history, philosophy, and practices.

- "The Dao De Jing" - Harvard University (Online Lecture): Harvard's online lecture series explores the "Dao De Jing," examining its historical context and philosophical significance. https://www.youtube.com/watch?v=pi9cnjEhXYY

Documentaries and Films:

- *Amongst White Clouds* (Documentary): This documentary offers a glimpse into the lives of Taoist hermits living in the Zhongnan Mountains of China, providing insights into their practices and perspectives.

- *The Taoist Wizard* (Film): A documentary film that explores Taoist practices and rituals, giving viewers a visual understanding of the tradition.

Taoist Organizations and Teachers:

• **Local Taoist Centers:** Many cities have Taoist centers or schools where you can attend classes, workshops, and events to learn from experienced practitioners.

• **Taoist Teachers:** Seek out teachings from contemporary Taoist teachers who may offer online courses, workshops, or written materials. Look for individuals with a solid background in Taoist philosophy and practices.

Additional Reading:

• **Journal Articles and Academic Papers:** Academic journals often publish articles on Taoism. JSTOR and other academic databases are good places to explore more scholarly writings.

• **Taoist Forums and Communities:** Engage with online forums and communities where practitioners and enthusiasts discuss Taoist philosophy, practices, and share resources.

Remember, Taoism is a diverse tradition, and exploring various perspectives can enhance your understanding. Whether you prefer classic texts, modern interpretations, or visual media, there are numerous resources to guide you on your journey into the depth of Taoist philosophy and practice.

Joining Taoist Communities and Gatherings

Embarking on a lifelong journey of understanding Taoism is a profound and enriching endeavor. Taoism, with its deep philosophical roots and practical wisdom, offers a unique perspective on life, relationships, and the natural order of the universe.

Here are some final words of encouragement before you embark up on your lifelong Taoism journey:

- **Embrace the Flow:** Taoism teaches the importance of going with the flow, adapting to the natural course of events, and embracing the inherent changes in life. As you explore Taoism, let this principle guide your journey. Embrace the fluidity of understanding and allow your insights to evolve over time.

- **Cultivate Inner Harmony:** The heart of Taoism lies in the cultivation of inner harmony. Take time to reflect, meditate, and nurture a sense of peace within yourself. The more you cultivate your inner landscape, the more attuned you become to the subtle currents of the Tao.

- **Explore Various Texts and Interpretations:** Taoism is rich with classical texts such as the "Tao Te Ching" and "Chuang Tzu," but there are also modern interpretations and commentaries. Explore various translations and perspectives to gain a holistic understanding of Taoist principles. Each interpretation may unveil new layers of wisdom.

- **Incorporate Taoist Practices:** Taoist practices, including meditation, qigong, and tai chi, offer tangible ways to embody Taoist principles. Integrate these practices into your daily life to experience the philosophy on a practical level. The physical and mental benefits can enhance your overall well-being.

- **Seek Guidance from Masters and Teachers:** Connect with experienced practitioners, teachers, or Taoist masters who can offer guidance and insights. Learning from those who have walked the path before you can provide valuable perspectives and deepen your understanding.

- **Celebrate the Yin-Yang Balance:** Taoism emphasizes the balance between Yin and Yang, the interplay of opposites. Recognize the dynamic equilibrium in all aspects of life. Celebrate the harmonious dance between contrasting forces and learn to find balance within the dualities.

- **Live Simply:** Taoism encourages a simple and uncluttered way of living. In your journey, simplify your life – both physically and mentally. Focus on what truly matters, let go of unnecessary complexities, and cultivate a sense of contentment in the present moment.

- **Appreciate Nature:** Nature is a central theme in Taoist philosophy. Spend time in nature, observe its rhythms, and draw inspiration from the natural world. Nature serves as a profound teacher, offering lessons about the cyclical nature of existence.

- **Practice Wu Wei in Daily Life:** The concept of Wu Wei, or non-action, suggests acting in accordance with the natural flow of events. Apply this principle in your daily life by allowing things to unfold organically, avoiding unnecessary resistance or force.

- **Be Patient and Open-Minded:** Understanding Taoism is a gradual process. Be patient with yourself and stay open-minded as you encounter new ideas and perspectives. The journey is about continuous learning and growth.

- **Share and Discuss:** Engage in discussions with fellow seekers, share your insights, and learn from the experiences of others. The communal exploration of Taoism can deepen your understanding and provide a supportive environment.

Remember that the journey of understanding Taoism is not about reaching a destination but about embracing the continuous flow of discovery and insight. Approach it with curiosity, humility, and a willingness to integrate its principles into your life. May your lifelong journey with Taoism bring you wisdom, peace, and a profound connection with the ever-unfolding Way.

References

The Biography of Lao Tzu |. https://sundaytimes.com.ng/biography-of-lao-tzu/

GPT4 Explains Econometrics: ": A Pioneering Force in the Evolution of Econometrics". https://causalinf.substack.com/p/gpt4-explains-econometrics-a-pioneering

Trend Archives - Tall Crooks. http://tallcrooks.com/category/trend/

Knowing and Exploring The Meaning Of Toioraljana - From Hunger To Hope. https://fromhungertohope.com/knowing-and-exploring-the-meaning-of-toioraljana/

Mental Health and Wellness: A Path to Inner Balance -. https://wurbal.in/mental-health-and-wellness-a-path-to-inner-balance/

The Yin Yang Diet and Yin Yang Foods - Souls Space. https://souls-space.com/yin-yang-diet-and-yin-yang-foods/

A Step-by-Step Guide to The Concept Of Yin Yang – WorldTrendz. https://www.worldtrendz.com/blogs/news/a-step-by-step-guide-to-the-concept-of-yin-yang

Yin and Yang: Understanding the Relationship - Easy Feng Shui. https://easy-fengshui.com/yin-and-yang-understanding-the-relationship-2/

What do we know about Chinese Dragons? EVERYTHING! - Dragon University. https://dragon.university/chinese-dragons/

Taoism: A Philosophy of Harmony and Balance | Evo4soul Multiversity. https://evo4soul.com/docs/taoism/

Chapter 4 of the Bhagavad Gita – Practical tips for life. https://bhaktimarga.ie/chapter-4-of-the-bhagavad-gita/

Meng, Qingyu. "Tao Te Ching : How Leaders Establish a Virtuous Circle of Non-action and Action : a Thesis Presented in Partial Fulfilment of the Requirements for the Degree of Master of Business Studies in Management at Massey University, Albany, New Zealand." 2022, https://core.ac.uk/download/547529333.pdf.

Rolex Day Date Ref. 1803 Circa 1968/9 – Walt Grace Vintage. https://waltgracevintage.com/products/rolex-day-date-wristwatch-ref-1803-circa-tbd

From Anthropologisch Theory to Real-Life Insights: Decoding Human Behavior | LittleArt Club. https://littleart.club/from-anthropologisch-theory-to-real-life-insights-decoding-human-behavior/

Housework Handled: Professional Cleaning Services for Your Home – Magimax Club. https://magimaxclub.net/housework-handled-professional-cleaning-services-for-your-home/

How to practice mindfulness in design • Swapnil Acharya. https://swapnilacharya.com/post/mindful-design/

Essay & Paragraph on Good Character » All Paragraph. https://allparagraph.com/character/

Painter Elizabeth Lennie's love for water showcased in Guelph-Humber Gallery | Humber News. https://humbernews.ca/2023/03/painter-elizabeth-lennies-love-for-water-showcased-in-guelph-humber-gallery/

Mental health strategies for a balanced life - Welcome to Perfecthealthsupply.com. https://perfecthealthsupply.com/mental-health-strategies-for-a-balanced-life/

Exploring The Immortal Peach Garden: A Mythical Journey Through Chinese Folklore. https://storiespub.com/immortal-peach-garden-story/

Explore 9 Effective Ways for Inner Peace and Serenity. https://astrotalk.com/astrology-blog/9-ways-to-find-inner-peace-and-serenity-insideastro-iatb8-7/

Acupuncture: Unlocking the Secrets of Meridians and Energy Flow – Horizon Healthcare. http://healthyheartrunwalk.com/acupuncture-unlocking-the-secrets-of-meridians-and-energy-flow/

Liu, Yinglu, and Shengyuan Yu. "Recent Approaches and Development of Acupuncture on Chronic Daily Headache." Current Pain and Headache Reports, 2015, https://doi.org/10.1007/s11916-015-0535-7.

Blonder, Lee X. "Historical and Cross-cultural Perspectives on Parkinson'S Disease." Journal of Complementary and Integrative Medicine, 2018, https://doi.org/10.1515/jcim-2016-0065.

7 Exercises for Strong Bones – Mountain Ice Pain Relief Gel. https://www.mountain-ice.com/pages/7-exercises-for-strong-bones

Best Meditation For Spiritual Awakening: Guided And Unguided. https://enhancedapp.io/meditation-for-spiritual-awakening

spinach Archives • My Family Fork. http://www.myfamilyfork.com/tag/spinach/

Outdoor Adventures for Middle Schoolers | Deer Hill Adventures. https://deerhillexpeditions.com/5-ways-to-build-the-connection-to-nature/

Intervals: Exploring the Musical Theory of Jose Carlos Matos – Jose Carlos Matos. https://josecarlosmatos.com/intervals/

The Impact of Inhaler Disposal on Our Environment - WealthInWastes. https://wealthinwastes.com/the-impact-of-inhaler-disposal/

Influencing Your Teen Without Trying to Control Them. https://counsellors.one/influencing-your-teen-without-trying-to-control-them/

Spiritual Wellbeing: Nourishing the Soul for a Fulfilling Life - Melpravda. https://melpravda.com/spiritual-wellbeing-nourishing-the-soul-for-a-fulfilling-life/

Simple Ways To Implement Mindfulness Into Your Relationship - HearthFeelings. https://hearthfeelings.com/web-stories/simple-ways-to-implement-mindfulness-into-your-relationship/

Unlock Success with Humility: The Entrepreneur's Guide to Growth. https://creoincubator.com/blog/humility-in-entrepreneurship-founders-guide

15 Best Ways To Improve Your Futuristic Thinking (2023). https://www.consultclarity.org/post/futuristic-thinking

How Self-Care Enhances Professional Performance. https://morgantaylormarketing.com/how-self-care-enhances-professional-performance/

Using Positive Intelligence to Promote Growth Mindset – University of San Diego - Professional & Continuing Education. https://pce.sandiego.edu/courses/using-positive-intelligence-to-promote-growth-mindset/

A Body of Water - Theatre reviews. https://chicagocritic.com/body-water/

10 Gardening basics for Beginners – TN Nursery. https://www.tnnursery.net/blogs/tn-nursery-blog/10-gardening-basics-for-beginners

thermal nature of people - CHINESE MEDICINE LIVING. https://www.chinesemedicineliving.com/tag/thermal-nature-of-people/

Feng shui means wind-water, NOT wind AND water. Here's why. - Feng Shui London UK • The Capital Feng Shui Consultant. https://www.fengshuilondon.net/feng-shui-means-wind-water-not-wind-and-water-heres-why/

Taoism: A Philosophy of Harmony and Balance | Evo4soul Multiversity. https://evo4soul.com/docs/taoism/

Srimad Bhagavad Gita | Luxe Edition | Bright Pink – ServDharm. https://servdharm.com/products/pink-bhagavad-gita

Chapter 4 of the Bhagavad Gita – Practical tips for life. https://bhaktimarga.ie/chapter-4-of-the-bhagavad-gita/

Psychodynamic Therapy, Mindfulness, Carl Rogers, Lao-Tzu, Cartesian Heritage, Psychotherapy, Ron Kurtz, Gestalt Theory, Taoist Theory, Buddhist Theories. Abaissement Theories, Bioenergetics Theories, Behavior Modification Principles, Rogerian Theory Principles, Character Theory Principles ⬜ Santa Barbara Deep Tissue - Riktr PRO Massage, Nicola, LMT. https://santabarbaradeeptissue.com/index.php/2023/08/18/psychodynamic-therapy-mindfulness-carl-rogers-lao-tzu-cartesian-heritage-psychotherapy-ron-kurtz-gestalt-theory-taoist-theory-buddhist-theories-abaissement-theories-bioenergetics-theories/

Lao Tzu Biography: Author of Tao Te Ching and founder of Taoism - Wiki. https://dsguruji.com/lao-tzu-biography-author-of-tao-te-ching-and-founder-of-taoism/

Yin and Yang: Understanding the Relationship - Easy Feng Shui. https://easy-fengshui.com/yin-and-yang-understanding-the-relationship-2/

From Anthropologisch Theory to Real-Life Insights: Decoding Human Behavior | LittleArt Club. https://littleart.club/from-anthropologisch-theory-to-real-life-insights-decoding-human-behavior/

Striking the Balance: Navigating Work-Life Harmony - Alt Attires. https://altattires.com/striking-the-balance-navigating-work-life-harmony/

Essay & Paragraph on Good Character » All Paragraph. https://allparagraph.com/character/

Painter Elizabeth Lennie's love for water showcased in Guelph-Humber Gallery | Humber News. https://humbernews.ca/2023/03/painter-elizabeth-lennies-love-for-water-showcased-in-guelph-humber-gallery/

Spiritual Passions: moonvisage: Location: Llandudno, United Kingdom. https://spiritualpassions.com/dating/moonvisage/

QiGong | CodedHealing. https://www.codedhealing.com/general-9-1

Ayurveda Treatments – Lanaoncospa. https://lanaoncospa.com/ayurveda/ayurveda-treatments/

Emotional Intelligence: Developing Soft Skills In Educators Through The IPGCE Program - IPGCE @ Derby. https://www.ipgce.com/emotional-intelligence/

ONEUP MULTIVERSE - CHOCOLATE MILK 4G - psychicstrains. https://psychicstrains.com/product/oneup-multiverse-chocolate-milk-4g/

Nurturing the Soul's Journey through Spirit Animals. https://www.therapybykathryn.com/blog/nurturing-the-souls-journey-through-spirit-animals

Unplug The Matrix, Change The Frequency - Real Estate Maui Blog. https://blog.realestatemaui.com/2015/02/01/unplug-the-matrix-change-the-frequency/

Brink Back Balance in Your Body with the Help of Ayurveda. https://shop.ayurythm.com/blog/Brink-Back-Balance-in-Your-Body-with-the-Help-of-Ayurveda

Change Management Training | Logos Leadership Development. https://logoslead.com/services/change-management/

Mindfulness for Navigating Life Transitions: Embracing Change with Grace - Divine You. https://divineyouwellness.com/blog/mindfulness-for-navigating-life-transitions-embracing-change-with-grace/

Qifang, He, and Canaan Morse. "Two Stories." Chinese Literature Today, 2010, https://doi.org/10.1080/21514399.2010.11833916.

NUMEROLOGY 7: LIFE PATH NUMBER 7 - Numerology Basics. https://numerologybasics.net/numerology-7-life-path-number-7/page/2/?et_blog

Navigating Life After College: A Guide for Graduates - College Aftermath. https://collegeaftermath.com/university/life-after-college/

Pramongkit, Prasopchoke, and Teay Shawyun. "Strategic IT Framework for Modern Enterprise by Using Information Technology Capabilities." 2003, https://doi.org/10.1109/iemc.2002.1038370.

Celebrating Success: Cloudwerx Named 2023 Google Cloud Sales Partner of the Year for North America. https://www.cloudwerx.tech/post/celebrating-success-cloudwerx-named-2023-google-cloud-sales-partner-of-the-year-for-north-america

Global Cybersecurity Market Reach USD 9,53,974.8 Mn by 2030. https://growthmarketreports.com/press-release/global-cybersecurity-market-reach-usd-9539748-mn-by-2030

7 Simple Zen Habits for a Stress-Free Life. https://www.aurahealth.io:443/blog/7-simple-zen-habits-for-a-stress-free-life

Health Skills Definition: A Pathway to a Fulfilling Life - careerscabin. https://careerscabin.com/health-skills-definition-a-pathway-to-a-fulfilling-life/

Cracking the Code: Strategies for Effective Affiliate Offer Promotions. https://dailycheddar.com/cracking-the-code-strategies-for-effective-affiliate-offer-promotions/

"Stoic Taoism: Modern Lessons from Ancient Philosophies" – A Timeless Guide to Thriving in the Modern World – Rhode Island Chronicle. http://news.rhodeislandchronicle.com/story/635151/stoic-taoism-modern-lessons-from-ancient-philosophies-a-timeless-guide-to-thriving-in-the-modern-world.html

ICSA Articles 3 - Taosim. https://articles3.icsahome.com/religion-showcase/taosim

The Taoist Classics: The Collected Translations of Thomas Cleary, Volume Three - Redwing Book Company. https://redwingbooks.com/product/taoclacle3/

9 798224 332281